Behind Many Doors

Edited by Phil Carradice and Briony Goffin

Published by Accent Press Ltd 2014

ISBN 9781783756247

The Whitchurch Project

The Whitchurch Project is a creative writing project that took place between 2007 and 2014. The project was administered by Literature Wales (formerly Academi), and led by writer and historian, Phil Carradice and writer and workshop facilitator, Briony Goffin.

With Whitchurch Hospital's closure on the horizon, the project was designed to give all those who have had a relationship with the hospital, whether they were service users, staff members, visitors, carers, or members of the local community, the opportunity to explore and express their experiences through creative writing. *Behind Many Doors* is a selection of the work that grew out of workshops, one-to-one writing sessions, interviews, as well as individual submissions.

The project was funded by Literature Wales and The Cardiff and Vale University Health Board (formerly the Cardiff and Vale NHS Trust).

Where appropriate, names have been changed to protect the identity and privacy of the people referred to in the following accounts.

Foreword

The World of Whitchurch

Each piece of writing in the following anthology offers its own luminous insight into the world of Whitchurch Hospital. Like a mosaic or stained-glass window, these fragments fit together to build a bigger dynamic picture of what Whitchurch Hospital has meant to all those who have experienced it. And, like a stained-glass window, each fragment allows us to glimpse hospital life through a particular lens and encounter different versions of the same world, each with its own atmosphere; each with its own truth.

Whitchurch Hospital is a fraught subject, beset with contradiction and associated with deep feeling. Across the project, our workshops and writing sessions endeavoured to create an environment which was safe and unbiased, to provide each writer the space to tell their own story, in their own words. Together, we would honour the courage to share and be witness, without judgment, to the imagery that surfaced.

For all of us present in the workshops, listening to each piece of writing was like being led around the hospital itself. Again and again, we were orientated by the water tower, disorientated by the corridors, and confronted with the repeated locking and unlocking of doors, in front of us and behind us. Echoes resounded through the empty channels of the building, rolling on from one piece to the next. Nature drew our gaze through the large un-opening windows, beating at the doors to get in, attempting to reclaim the building for itself; and hinted at the possibility of fertility, offering moments of light and respite amidst the density of trauma and illness.

These works also led us on a journey through a world of paradox. Whitchurch Hospital, all at once, appeared to represent rescue and abandonment, safety and entrapment, protection and vulnerability, healing and suffering. Even the architecture straddled a sense of beauty and grotesquery – the 'ghastly splendour' of the entrance hall, the 'unsafe refuge' of the wards. From the seam of that conflict, writing emerged that was complex, nuanced, and very real – 'the flowery sofas, dirty yet so inviting'.

The accumulation of writing became a myriad of different voices, each one adding to the surface area of the history and mythology of the hospital. From this multiplicity of perspective, singular motifs began to form. A sense of the 'closed' or 'containing' nature of the institution, as embodied through references to prison, concentration camps, a zoo, a holding pen; a sense of the self-sustaining, world-all-of-its-own, with comparisons to a planet, a spaceship, an ocean liner; and a sense of otherness or 'set apartness' as invoked through fairy-tale castles. All these images are characterised by feelings of inside and outside, being tethered or cast adrift, belonging or not belonging.

Then there were the ghosts we encountered. Amidst all these voices are allusions to those who have gone before, those whose traces remain still in the blood stains, the graffiti, the sprawling plants in the greenhouse, the dust in the light beams, the whispering in the corridors. There are repeated references to what the walls have borne witness to and what the fabric of the hospital has absorbed over a century and more.

In some cases, the building felt as if it had its own breath, its own heartbeat – 'I loved it … it loved me too'. The hospital as a live being seemed to develop out of a sense of reciprocal relationship between the individual and the space they inhabited. The building joins with the person and the person joins with the building – 'you begin to stagnate, your lungs fall into step … while you fuse gently with the carpet.' A shared narrative formed that, ultimately, makes it impossible to separate a building from its ghosts. Even when the people are long gone, this place will be synonymous with its history and those who passed through its doors.

Then there are the ghosts we will all take away with us. Whitchurch Hospital gets under the skin and seeps into the layers of consciousness – 'the memories of those corridors stay with me all the time' – 'the memories of those lives have touched me, informed me of what it means to be human, and remained in my thoughts to this day' – 'I never returned to Whitchurch, only in my dreams.' This writing is testimony to the pervasiveness of Whitchurch Hospital, that even if we never enter the grounds again, or step upon the sequence of shallow stone steps to the entrance hall, or wander the great arc of corridor, Whitchurch has embedded itself in the mind.

Sometimes psychiatric hospitals feel like secret worlds, enshrouded in mystery and rumour, regarded with trepidation; particularly those old redbrick institutions – the iconic gothic structure, beheld from afar, set alone amidst sweeping grounds and broad mature trees. *The Whitchurch Creative Writing Project* sought to shine light on that world, from the point of view of those who have lived it, whether they were patients, staff, visitors, carers, or members of the local community. Their impressions and their anecdotes, their poetry and their prose, create vivid testimony to a complex world, and combine to create a multifaceted picture of a hospital and of psychiatric medicine, as given, as received, as witnessed, as imagined, as experienced across the twentieth and into the twenty-first century. Together, these writers have produced a meaningful and moving legacy that not only offers intimate, historical insight into a particular world but could even assist in the way we think about the nature of hospitals, psychiatry, and the provision of holistic mental healthcare in the future.

Briony Goffin
Workshop facilitator – The Whitchurch Project

Memory Minute to Minute

I arrive at 11 at night, my son has been sick in my hair, on my clothes, in the car and my husband drops me at the door and leaves. The lobby is dark and empty and the receptionist shows me a bare room where I sit and see through a painting where people are speaking still they're in the hospital even and nobody knows because I have let them in when I opened the door they say you were going to do it, you should be in prison and I curl up safe because alone in this room I can do nothing.

The doctor comes says how do you feel, safe I tell her, safe. I tell her about the witch-woman at the top of the ladder, banging her fists and screaming and the hospital is full. We'll have to treat her at home. My husband tells them he can't, the baby is sick and the children will be scared. There's a taxi and a nurse who's pissed off at her easy shift being broken she doesn't want to get in a taxi in the cold the taxi driver sees a crazy middle-aged woman and I don't mind for once, I just watch what's it to him or me the nurse gives some notes in a brown envelope to the night nurse and she says I'm going I don't even know this patient the night nurse is so young she gives me anti-psychotics you'll sleep until the morning thank god I don't take off my clothes or lock the door but the tranquilisers last two hours.

Back at Whitchurch I walk to ECT and wheel back, the same each time until my brain is blurred and I can't remember from one minute to the next ECT, lie on the sofa where I'm an outsider, drug myself and try to sleep, crisis house, student room, tiny kitchen, television, tiny life, contained, walled in thank god. I don't have to speak I don't have to move. Except to go and buy more sleeping tablets and caffeine. How ridiculous but how fitting for a bipolar to treat herself with opposites. Pulling both ways!

Romy Wood

Living on the Edge 1

Growing up in the shadow of Whitchurch Hospital, I observed the water tower from my bedroom window, an ever-present reminder of the secret place, the healing place, the asylum for mad people.

Fear abounds that the hospital wards are no longer locked – lock up your children instead, keep them safe from the mad people, they are dangerous. One patient escapes and runs down our street in her night dress and slippers. Her freedom is short-lived as two men in white coats guide her back. She looks frightened and distressed. They are firm and authoritative. I am ushered indoors. I ask youthful questions about what is happening. No one answers me.

A teenager now and I am more used to these strange apparitions that appear in my neighbourhood. One such is a man who believes that he is a train. 'Tommy the train' wears a cap and has a stick under his arm and has a whistle in his mouth. He runs up and down Pendwyallt Hill journeying somewhere in his mind that is incomprehensible to the rest of us. Nothing detracts him from his task, taunts do not deter him.

The grounds have always attracted me. The church is a symbol of a spiritual resting place amidst the chaos of mind. The summer houses, adorned with garlands of flowers, look beautiful. The bowling green is manicured to perfection, and in the background the sound of leather on willow echoes in the summer air as the local cricket team play their leisurely game.

Nature brings its healing touch to this place. But all too

soon the fantasy is pierced by the sounds of manic voices, controlling voices, shuffled activity. Peace is resumed, but the illusion is revealed. There is no enduring peace here – only moments.

And now in my early twenties, I work in the Occupational Therapy Department at the hospital. Here, I am to be part of a team of helpers organising salvation for the sick in the form of work. I am given a tour of the hospital in my induction. Finally I understand that the tower of my childhood nightmares is a water tower and never has or could have the function that was part of my early education. I am shown the underground tunnels, a vast world in its own right. I shudder at the secrets such a place undoubtedly holds, of those tortured souls who disappeared into the bowels of their own eternity.

I am shown the wards which spindle out from the semi-circular corridor that forms the main access route through the hospital. This horseshoe shape suggests to me a good-luck talisman for all who enter. The wards attempt to convey a sense of home, the nursing staff a sense of family care, where the original has ceased to do so.

I am offered an opportunity to witness a patient undergoing ECT treatment. Sedated and then strapped to the bed, I watch as the current enters a human body, causing it to writhe and arc until the electrical dose has been fully delivered. I watch the body slump as the straps are loosened and the patient left to sleep. I am told that his short-term memory will be affected, that they don't really know how what they are doing to him works, but that it might. I am reminded of the neurologists who used to remove and dissect brain parts to the same ends. I still cannot fail to feel revulsion.

Ruth Hawkins

The Giant's Back

I am in the corridor again – arched like the spine of a sleeping giant – and I am alone. The client I am visiting has been sectioned. His world, briefly expanded, has once again shrunk. He smokes cigarettes in a large green cage and reminisces about the feel of his feet on pavements and the joy of cups of tea in cafés. In his garden is a broken greenhouse where plants once tried to grow.

I am a ferry service between the outside world and the inner. Down this corridor I transport information and news, letters and encouragement. Every week I pass the forlorn and faded plastic chairs put out to grass and framed by cobwebbed windows, the scrawled words in messy biro on pink walls never to be re-painted, the overflowing bins. I tread the lino flooring designed to hide stains and wear well.

Nothing here speaks to me of wellness, or recovery, or future. Nothing here says home and every time I come here I hope that one day we will make the journey back to the car park, and the sun, together.

Emma Musty

Falling

I came to Whitchurch Hospital isolated from the world: my world and the greater world. My entire mind and body had gone into shock after being raped by a neighbour four months previously. I had not been touched – not hugged, not comforted, not connected – in any way for these months. My memory of touch was the giant swabs, the 'please lie on your stomach' and the cutting of my hair for all the tests, tests of endurance, at the police station afterwards.

I sat there from day one, on the end of my bed in the women's dormitory (one of the last of its kind) flicking through magazines that visitors who I'd wished would just leave had brought me. What did I need with *Cosmo*, *Glamour*, and *Company*? The people in the pages, their glaringly white teeth and latest fashions, meant nothing to me, even the aspirational sneakiness of advertising failed to reach me and make me, well, aspire.

There were curtains around the beds and I did constant battle with nursing assistants to keep mine closed. Every bit of privacy and solitude was craved for. They didn't care; it was ward policy in the day time.

They made it clear that they thought I was a burnt-out university student, poor little rich girl. I was desperate but far from rich. Two weeks after arriving my class graduated. My Mother still hadn't phoned to find out if I was walking in a cap and gown or taking sedatives and trying to read magazines.

I wrote on my stomach with a biro 'DO NOT TOUCH'.

'Hey Ruby, do you feel like taking a nap?' came the

voice through the closed curtain that was usually swished open without announcement. 'Yeah, I really do,' I replied, wondering what the catch was in my need actually being recognised.

Later I got up and that voice was serving dinner. 'What's that?' I said as I pointed at the jumble of chunks in one of the deep trays on the heated metal serving station.

'Goulash,' I was assured. I ate my plateful and dutifully (always a stickler for the rules) placed my crockery on the metal wheeled tea tray.

'So Ruby, what was it?' said the voice who now had a face, a kind face.

'Er, goulash?'

'Oh phew,' came the response. I smiled for the first time in four months. In the process of forming what became a dinner time in-joke she had made a connection with me through the barbed fence I had pulled on like a cloak.

Days dragged on as I was told over and over that 'there's no overnight cure'. I didn't need to be told this, I was good at waiting, so long as they kept me here. I didn't think I'd be able to stand the noise and light out there, beyond the water tower and the bowling green.

For a few days I got a 'Hey Ruby' through my closed curtains when she was working. Those 'Hey Ruby's became a lifeline, a tiny stepping stone between myself and humanity. Between total isolation and a centrifugal force around which my time spun.

The seasonal sunshine struck my tired head in striped beams through the Victorian windows above my single hospital bed. When they had been lifted up in order for the sanitation workers to clean underneath the usually mute patient in the next cubicle said 'That's the most action these beds will ever see'. But I digress. Yes, the sun shone on my tired head and the long hair attached, now a shoddy mix of black (I had dallied with the goth look) and the light ginger that I had tried to dye away.

Then the voice and the face at the curtain. 'Ruby, got any plans this afternoon?' The very notion that I had plans for any afternoon was laughable.

'Ha! Why?'

'Well I noticed your friend brought you in that hair dye on your shelf, want me to dye your hair?'

A nurse, asking if she could dye my hair? All the little 'Hey Ruby's' had built up into an affinity. I ventured to say yes.

She touched my hair, my head, and occasionally, accidentally my ears. The chemical smell did not detract from the sensation of the human touch, no matter how vain, superficial, and fleeting. She tied my hair in a bun and told me the time so I'd know when to wash it off.

Twenty minutes later she came back and we joked about the damage we'd done with staining drips on the avocado bath suite in the dated ward. Time for the rinse off.

The shower head was attached above the tap end of the bath. Even though I'm 5'6 and a half (the half being important growing up in a tall family) and the nurse whom I had now been calling my 'Walking Valium' being about the same we couldn't reach it.

Ever the practical thinker I solved the problem immediately. I would simply put down the toilet lid, stand on it, and unhook the shower head from its lofty residence on the far wall.

The next two seconds of my life happened in slow motion. I heard a crack. The middle of the toilet lid gave way. I fell straight downwards. My toes got wet then my whole foot. My arse hit the floor. My foot felt soaked. And there I remained. My 'Walking Valium' was laughing so hard she could barely stay upright. If I hadn't already been on the floor I would have ended up there in silent heaving guffaws. We laughed so loud that other patients came to the bathroom door and two other nursing staff had arrived out of breath with the emergency suicide first aid kit. And they laughed. And the patients laughed. I let go, I felt it deep within me, a release that combined Sod's Law and fantastic human self-depreciating awareness.

For the rest of my admission I talked to my 'Walking Valium' whenever she was on shift. Going against staff protocol she would hug me occasionally. At first this repulsed me … why would anyone want to touch such a violated girl? By the end of my stay I was hugging her back, talking about my plans to get a flat and start over, perhaps even get a car.

However, something was burning on my mind.

Sometime later I was being questioned by a man in a boiler suit and high visibility jacket for the mandatory health and safety report. Something greater than blaming poor construction, outdated facilities, and possible preventative negligence was heckling every waking thought.

I stopped him and I tentatively, whilst looking at the floor, asked the question that had been tormenting me ever since my *salle-de-bain folie*.

'Was it flushed?' I uttered.

'Er, let me just check the accident scene report,' he said as he lifted sheets of paper on his clipboard.

'Yes,' came the most glorious answer I had ever had the delight to welcome into my ears.

Ruby Holmes

If it weren't for me …

There's a crumpled, greying photograph of my uncle in the family album: flying gear, pipe in hand, slightly receding hairline. You can tell from his stance and open face that he was happy. But all I remember is a hospital room, and an iron bed – and me aged about ten sitting beside not knowing whether I ought to be scared, even with my parents there. He seemed a kindly man, though such a ghost of one that I do not remember even *seeing* him: he was as faded as the photograph.

Is happiness so fragile? What does it take to make it go away? The war, I suppose. He was a navigator with a pathfinder squadron. They were the ones who went out in Lancaster bombers to find German targets for bombing raids. Their job was to guide in the bombers or report back on gun emplacements and so forth. I think you would have to be a very good navigator to do that, but he must have felt small and vulnerable up there in the sky. Another target for someone to aim at.

He was not the same after that. He went home to live with his parents after the war, but one day he snapped. A danger to someone, they said. Safer for him to stay in the album; keep him there. His family – my family – did not reject him, they just did not understand.

One man's fear is another man's paranoia, and so mental illness can be born. They would probably call it Post Traumatic Stress Disorder these days. They did not then. They called it Schizophrenia and sectioned him. He was there in Whitchurch Hospital for many years. More than twenty, I think. It's a long time to sit around believing you are mad. Rehabilitation meant moving into a hostel and making simple furniture, along with other ex-patients. It did not mean going home.

If it weren't for me, my parents said, he could have come and lived with us. If it weren't for my cousins, my aunts and uncles said, he could have lived with them. If it weren't for the war, well, if it weren't for the war, who knows?

I do not remember what he died of. Lack of love, probably.

Gill Jones

Relapse

There is a commotion outside the front doors again.

I walk towards the office used for assessing patients, which is situated on my left at the beginning of a long corridor; the corridor that leads to the heavy double doors of Whitchurch Hospital.

I wonder whether I should go and assist or just wait. I decide I can best use my time by finding some paper to write on, and hurriedly pull open all the drawers in the desk, one by one, to find something suitable.

The noise is louder now, there are sounds of commanding voices, and as I hear many footsteps approach, there is a delayed clang as the front door closes: the entourage has arrived. Four policemen, two heavy set and the others of medium build, towering over and frog marching a skinny young man who looks petrified.

The black hair of this lad was spiky and dishevelled. He wore a striped T-shirt and his jacket and trousers looked as if they belonged to someone who had eaten much better than he had in the previous weeks. With gaunt pale cheeks and dry cracked lips his eyes showed only fear.

The motley group came to a stop before me in the examination room which now seemed too small for purpose. I looked at the young man and smiled to try to reassure him. His arms were trembling slightly. To my horror I suddenly realised why one of the officers was standing so close – he was handcuffed to my patient – and not only that, but they had chosen to do so on the side the lad had tried to cut his wrist. Anger and pity welled inside of me.

All was suddenly quiet with the six of us standing there. The lad bowed his head and a few drops of blood dripped from his fingers onto the floor.

Dr Elizabeth Thomas

East 2A

Was it a dodgy mirror? she asked herself. She wasn't sure. She glanced up again as she passed the little old woman sat in the chair beneath the mirror picking at her toes. Yes her face did look slightly lopsided on the left side in this mirror.

'My feet are too small,' said the old woman.

'No they're not, mine are smaller.' She replied. The thought occurred to her that if she carried on with this conversation she'd need an extra diazepam pretty soon.

She made her way to the smoke room, passing the toilets, the solitary shower and bathroom, for the use of sometimes twenty patients, each with differing degrees of mental illness or dementia. Next she passed the laundry room with its insistent, whirring noise, and through the T.V. lounge to the dining area. She noticed the tea trolley; you don't need a watch in Whitchurch Hospital, you can tell the time by the tea trolley, where its magical appearance signifies breakfast, lunch, dinner, and supper with pinpoint accuracy. She paused to collect her tea. Which stained plastic cup should she use, green, yellow, or red? She chose yellow. She shuffled on towards the locked ward door next to which was the smoke room.

All lighters being confiscated, an electric car cigarette lighter had been installed in the small room. She'd tried to regulate her smoking but in here it was either T.V. lounge or smoke room; time becomes slower, it dawdles along on Ward East 2A.

Noises seem to rise to another level in E2A, the doorbell rings constantly, a loud rattling sound and after a while you no longer jump when you hear it. Added to this, someone regularly sets off the fire alarm, which has a sharp stinging tone, and everyone ambles to the dining area. She often thought that if there ever was a real fire nobody would ever get out, because no firemen ever attend Whitchurch.

On her way back from the smoke room she knocked at the door of the nurses' station and asked for the bath plug and for her razor from the locked treatment room. She understood about the razor, although she had an intense fear of being given someone else's razor, and always tried to make sure it was her name on the bag, but what injury could be inflicted with a rubber plug she was never quite sure.

Today she'd seen her consultant and had been told with impeccable politeness, that the tablets she was taking to combat the side effects in themselves had side effects, blurred vision being one, and the more she thought about it, she was glad she hadn't reported the dodgy mirror.

Tomorrow she was going home and had packed up her belongings in preparation for a whole day of never knowing when you would be allowed to go, after they'd collected medication, waited for the crisis team to deem you fit to be taken on, etc.

Then it would be time to trek along the seemingly endless stone corridors, with their deafening echoes and traffic mirrors, for the corridors are wide enough for small laundry trucks to travel through. On to the reception area with its large wooden desk almost as tall as she was, out through the double doors and under the stone archway back into the twenty-first century, she would see the water tower which was a relic from another age, like the place itself. When it was thought prudent to keep the patients' water separate from that of the staff for fear of contamination.

When Whitchurch locks its doors for the final time,

there will be a small proportion of people for whom it has become home. These people will be foisted onto an already over-stretched community service. The vast majority, however, will raise a glass to its demise and hope that the opportunity is now taken to move the mental health teams based there into a more modern and user-friendly working environment.

Theresa Ann Gallivan

Jack and Lilly

I stop for a moment and read the inscriptions, 'Edward Hain, Captain Royal of 1st Devon Yeomanry; Second Lieutenant W. H. Seagar of the 10th South Wales Borderers; and the Captain, Officers and Crew of S.S Dulverton – lost at sea in 1907.'

Their memory is etched on the brass plaques and wooden frames that line this part of the corridor. The walls on which they hang bear faded white paint. They continue on down past locked doors and cracked window panes where the glazed glass lets light in, but offers no view outside. There is nothing else here and the slightest of sounds echo around this stiff place. Here and there, mirrors parked high up on walls survey the empty corridors and I sense the shadows of those who came here on their journey to renewal.

Years ago this corridor was the scene of stretchers, men with bandaged heads, doctors in straight, white coats in full stride, and nurses pushing the injured in wheelchairs to and from Theatre. It was the scene of both medical and military uniforms, the clothing of those protecting and serving each other.

Jack was one of the lucky ones. He arrived in 1940 after a leg injury sustained during battle in France. Many of his comrades were rescued after the German advance, yet many more never made it – captured or killed in action. But Jack was strong. At 6'2 he was well framed, and bigger than most other soldiers. Not only did he stand out amongst the Argyll and Sutherland Highlanders, but also in the hospital ward where his presence was unavoidable to the young nurses who bathed his wounds and dressed his stitched up skin.

He told animated stories about boat trips to the Orkney Isles where he would fish in the clearest of blue seas – falling in and wading back to shore for a dram of whisky by the fire at the local inn. His charm was served up in great helpings to the patients and nurses at Whitchurch Hospital. While on their tea break the nurses would laugh and chatter between themselves about the handsome, blue-eyed giant on West Ward 4.

Lilly had seen him too. She was the ward sister and had relocated to Whitchurch after completing her training in Plymouth. The city was getting heavily bombed so she headed back home to Wales where she enrolled at the hospital, nursing hundreds of servicemen back to health. Jack's Scottish lilt had caught Lilly's attention during her rounds. At the end of each shift, she would hang back in the tiled corridor, peering through the ward window to catch a glimpse of him.

Being far from home, Jack had no visitors and this made Lilly sad. So when letters arrived for him, she would take them to him, reading them aloud and commenting on the beautiful handwritten notes from his mother. She brought him some of her own notepaper so he too could correspond and she began scribing the words that he dictated.

As Jack recovered and his leg became stronger, he started to walk up and down the corridor. On his strolls he would stop and talk to passers by and wink at Lilly, who was behind the counter, preparing patients' files for the doctors' rounds. Later, she invited him for a walk in the hospital grounds, she relaying childhood tales with seven siblings in Pontypridd and he expressing hopes of returning to Scotland and finding a sweetheart.

Soon, the other nurses noticed that Lilly was showing a special interest in Jack and they confronted her, saying,

'Are you flirting with him hoping you will be the one he chooses?'

'Yes,' she told them. 'I bags him. He's mine.'

The day Jack was discharged from the hospital there had been an influx of wounded soldiers. The hustle of people and equipment in the corridors made it difficult for him to find Lilly. He knew she would be busy, but he had to see her.

Jack sat on a wooden bench in the hospital grounds. He sat there for hours gazing at the church on the far side and the bell tower with its pale green dome perched on top. He thought about Lilly and how she must have looked after many service men who would have also been enamoured by her warm-hearted nature and delicate features. Yet, he continued to wait and at 10 p.m. he went back inside and wandered down the corridor to see if she had finished her shift. Everything was much quieter now and he stopped for a moment outside the matron's office. There was a leaflet pinned to a notice-board advertising a dance at the local church hall.

As he read, the door opened and Lilly emerged from behind it, carrying her nursing cape and bag. Now she was standing before him, he didn't know what to say to her. She looked pleased to see him yet he shifted on his feet, smoothed back his parted hair with his hand, and asked her, 'Do you like dancing?' He pointed at the leaflet on the notice-board, becoming aware of how loudly he had spoken.

With a blushed cheek, Lilly firmly replied, 'Yes. I do.'

Today, the echo of this invitation still resonates across the corridor. Now, it is louder than ever as I, Jack and Lilly's granddaughter, remember them. I stand in the corridor for a little while longer and brushing my hand over the plaques of the fallen, I wonder what other stories this place could tell.

Rhiannon Morgan

History Snapshot 1

Until the second half of the nineteenth century, in Britain as in many other supposedly developed countries, there was very little help for people who were mentally ill. In the eyes and minds of the general public, mental health problems – insanity as they would have called it – were firmly linked with poverty and, in many cases, with crime.

In the seventeenth, eighteenth, and early nineteenth centuries, people with the wealth and means to do so had been able to care for family members with mental health problems by the simple act of hiring professional carers – although quite how 'professional' such people were remains a matter of conjecture. Often mentally ill people were locked away, out of sight and memory, sometimes for years until death eventually took a hand – the sad but fictional case of Mrs Rochester in Charlotte Bronte's Jane Eyre is a classic example.

An alternative was to pay for admission into a private asylum where the quality of care was minimal and treatment, in general, non-existent. Such establishments did not come cheap but they were there if people chose to look.

For the poor, however, provision was even more sketchy. There were a small scattering of 'public hospitals for the insane' but it was more a case of luck than judgment if one happened to be located within fifty miles of your home. For most people the only option was the hated workhouse. Or, preferably, containment within their own village where people who knew them and understood their problems would help to contain and console.

From the middle years of the century, however, as the effects of the Industrial Revolution really began to bite, it was clear that there would have to be wholesale change in the provision.

The Industrial Revolution meant the breakdown of many rural environments as the population became increasingly geographically mobile with families decamping to the industrial belts of England and Wales. Urban environments began to double or even treble in size, almost literally overnight. And, of course, social and emotional problems that had previously been contained within the village or town became suddenly exaggerated as the delicate fabric of society came under direct or, often, dimly perceived threat.

As with criminals and the unemployed, people with mental health problems found themselves increasingly stigmatized. They were, it was felt, a threat to the social stability of the country, although there was no proof of any such contention. But in a society where the doctrine of 'Self Help,' as outlined by Samuel Smiles, soon assumed almost religious significance, the very fact that they could not help themselves quickly made them dispensable.

As a consequence, it was thought, people with significant mental health difficulties needed to be gathered up and locked away in secure environments where they could no longer cause problems or disruption.

And what that way of thinking led to was the creation of large institutions where the emphasis was more on containment than on treatment. It meant, in effect, the emergence of the classic Victorian asylum.

Phil Carradice
Author, historian, and lead writer on The Whitchurch Project

Tower

I live within sight of the hospital. I have always noticed the tower, right from when I was a child, the tower more than anything else.

My father used to say if I ever got lost, make my way towards the tower. It was a homing device – in the days when you didn't have such things. Look for the tower, he'd say, it'll guide you home.

Anonymous

Fire Response

Following a dreadful fire in the early 1970s at Farleigh Hospital outside Bristol, which caused the deaths of many elderly and long-stay patients, plus a spate of fires at other UK mental hospitals, there was an overhaul of fire procedures – equipment, training, etc., at Whitchurch as elsewhere.

Access to alarm points was opened to include patients. This meant that many long-established ways of dealing with false and nuisance alarm calls, together with the reduction in security arrangements, led inevitably to a rapid increase in inappropriate alarm use.

The fire brigade was initially enthusiastic. Hospital staff no longer tried to extinguish fires themselves, even though the hospital was very well equipped with plenty of hydrants, hoses, and various cylinders. Staff were directed to concentrate on removing and checking patients and focusing on assembly points, etc.

The brigade would usually turn up in a long procession of tenders, including disaster wagons and special vehicles with hot soup and blankets.

After about two years of an enormous number of attention-seeking false alarms we noticed a certain cynicism among the firemen and a senior fire officer confided that he was having difficulty in getting some of the chaps to strap themselves into their anti-smoke gear when the destination 'Whitchurch' was announced.

One particular senior fireman was keen on turning all false alarm calls into full, major fire drills, which would include all patients, all staff, and visitors.

This was impossible, of course, and led to argument and upset and inevitable souring of relationships.

Part of the problem was the installation of a super-sensitive fire detection system which would be set off for no apparent reason several times a day.

The fire service felt that staff were not doing enough to prevent unnecessary call-outs and hospital staff felt that the fire service were expecting the impossible. Eventually, however, an actual and quite serious ward fire, which was started by a recently discharged patient and which could have become a major incident, was handled well by the staff of both services and led to mutual congratulation and the return of normal relations.

Keith Sullivan

Living on the Edge 2

And so I begin my work as an Occupational Therapy Aide. Patients are referred here as a result of case conference decisions for rehabilitation. Carl is schizophrenic, he tells me. Whatever that means to him and his psychiatrist I find that he is a mild-natured, cheerful man in his twenties, for whom life has dealt a cruel family. His response is to find an alternative world to inhabit, with imaginary humans of his own design; his private world. He brings sunshine to my working day and laughter to the workshop.

He will soon be leaving the hospital, going back to live with his family. He has responded well to treatment; he is stable. He hopes to get a job and spends his time in the department working conscientiously on the industrial therapy line. I am hopeful for him. He is less so. He has another label; he is called a 'revolving door' type of patient. Discharged back to his family, employment rarely lasts long before his symptoms return and his condition deteriorates. His family cease to manage him and don't want him there and so he returns to the hospital.

Over the years since he started coming here as a teenager he has woven baskets and footstools, and tried all the new therapies on offer. As a result of an 'incident' (never talked about), he is considered too risky to use wood-working tools and is banned from the carpentry workshop. His attempts at art have so far been short-lived. However, music therapy offers him sanctuary and peace in an otherwise turbulent mind. I am too young and naïve to appreciate how psychiatry is unable to fix his life, even if the drugs are able to dampen his mental creations.

Irene lives in the community and visits as a day patient. Her paranoia abates, but she is still bird like, ever watchful, scanning others for treacherous actions. She stays close to the other day patients on the assembly line, careful to convey her status as one who is sane and who will leave the hospital at the end of the day.

Tony shuffles in with the use of a walking stick. Alcohol misuse over too many years has affected the nerves in his legs. He has also suffered a stroke so that his speech is slurred and it has created paralysis in his arm and other leg. In spite of it all he likes nothing more than to regale of drinking times past. In his mind alcohol has always been and continues to be his friend. He remains oblivious to the facts of a broken marriage, children he never sees, a life of poverty and ill health. He remains deluded by the great seducer, alcohol.

Andy is a manic depressive with psychopathic tendencies. The first time I meet him I am already half an hour into an intelligent conversation with him about nursing care at the hospital, before I realise that he isn't the charge nurse that he says he is, alerted as I am by the OT supervisor. She guides me to the office under some pretext. I am confused, I do not understand these illnesses; I don't know if I am in danger; I don't know if we are all in danger, and I am angry. The real charge nurse from the ward arrives to take him back. He has used his guile to leave the ward unnoticed.

The next time I see him I don't recognise him. He has once again freed himself from the ward, though the nurse is closer on his tail than before. Andy is in his pyjamas and slippers. His hair is dishevelled. His eyes are wide and wild. He is ranting; the mania has taken hold faster than the medication. I am frightened by him as are the other patients in the room. They cower and become distressed, triggered into their own nightmare worlds. Then as swiftly as he arrives, he is gone and 'peace' resumes. But the silence hangs filled with menace and I once again feel a mix of sadness and bewilderment at what is going on here.

Ruth Hawkins

Local Hero

The worried look had always been there.

Growing up in a small terraced house in the middle of Cardiff, on a main road, noise of the traffic in the front, the railway at the back. Sandwiched between was the rifle range, and a small alleyway that led to the back lane.

Living in our house were grandparents, mother, Uncle Bernie, and me; I am about five years old. I can still picture this humble house.

Uncle Bernie returned from the Second World War, a Burma veteran.

He was ragged to say the least, he looked like a picture that you saw of Jesus. Long grey unkempt hair and beard, ragged clothes and old boots. He played the saxophone, which from a five-year-old's point of view made horrible noises. Looking back it was his only pleasure. He would walk the lanes through each season, early spring days, he would listen to the sound of the birds and watch the flowers and trees beginning to bloom. In summer time longer walks, watching our garden change with bright flowers and their fragrance, the night scented with jasmine and honeysuckle. Autumn with the leaves changing colour, the way the breeze blew through the days, through to winter and the extra scarf being worn, the rhythm of our life was endless.

He never mentioned the war except he had served in the Burma campaign, and was lost in the jungle. His mental condition deteriorated, thus the journey to Whitchurch Hospital began. The diagnosis was religious mania. My uncle could recite the Bible chapter and verse.

One journey as a child, I can walk through it as if it was yesterday, Uncle Bernie was an inpatient in the hospital, when we were due to visit him. On a cold December day with our winter coats, scarves, and mittens keeping us warm, my mother, sister, and myself made our way to the bus stop near Cardiff Central Station. The bus came to a stop by the open-air fruit market in The Hayes, the paraffin lamps shone through the cold mist of this December day and lit the colourful produce. The sight and smell of the roast chestnuts, we were allowed a small bag which we shared as we walked along to the next part of our trip.

An unfamiliar part of Cardiff that I had never ventured into, the road seemed extra wide from our vantage point on the top deck. The street lights shone through the fog. We arrived at our destination: Whitchurch Hospital. It seemed foreboding, as we stood by the wrought-iron gate, searching the grounds. The building looked austere, with its red bricks and large tower hosting a green roof. I assume now that it was to be used in case an inmate would try to escape. Pushing the gates open, making our way to the main door of the hospital. Once inside, long corridors with wards sprouting from them.

Noises from the wards, shouting, screaming, with doctors and nurses walking swiftly to help with the rumpus that came from these wards.

Eventually we reached the ward where Uncle Bernie was. A stern nurse asked who we had come to see. This explained, we were shown to his bedside.

The visit was not very long, but the ward had been decorated for Christmas; I stared at the ceiling where coloured stars as large as saucers glinted down on the hospital ward. A Christmas tree in the corner, with handmade decorations, made from paper and cardboard, paper lanterns of bright orange, reds and greens adorned the tree. Paper chains hung at precarious angles, it seemed a less clinical atmosphere. The visit being over, at the sound of a bell, we trooped out of the ward, along the corridor.

There was a sign which announced a sale of work to raise funds for the hospital. Volunteers had knitted hats, scarves, mittens, at the corner of the table a knitted rag doll. Oh, I wanted this rag doll so much, money being very scarce especially as Christmas was fast approaching.

The journey home was one of excitement. On my lap was the rag doll, a favourite toy for many years.

My uncle never recovered from his mental state, and died of cancer in Sully Hospital in 1972, an unsung hero, who had been forgotten.

Jeanette Edwards

Your Hold on Me

Visit 1

I arrived by bus, can't remember which one. It was late afternoon, a lifeless wet day to match my mood. I'd probably miss tea, still after overeating for the past few days it would be good to skip a meal. I was sure I'd get away with it. The ward door was locked. It would become known to me, what everyone else already knew it as, the lock-up ward. Intensive Care Unit was its official title. When the next door was locked I knew; this was serious.

I never realised things could have got so bad. I recognised signs – even told tutors at college my fears, but actually walking in to the bedroom, seeing dots of stained blood on the door, I was scared. Didn't stay long. Little did I know. Little did I know I'd be back. Back to visit yet another friend in that place. Your hold on me had begun.

Visit 2

This time my parents drove me there. Dad was not allowed to come in with me. Mom forbade him. It was a gorgeous sunny September morning. Had that first day back at school feel – the familiar chill to the air filled with forthcoming fear and anxiety. I even *felt* like a kid; the odd one out.

Night was the worst, having to walk through that corridor of darkness not knowing what was lurking behind the curtains. You could hear snores from some beds, crying from others, but it was the silent ones that bothered me the most. Were there men there at all, were they watching me, maybe they were about to jump on me? But what about the nurses? Where were they? Their office felt so much further away at night.

I only stayed two weeks. I felt so desperate yet how could they say my time was over. I couldn't cope – I needed that place. Having to face my demons alone. How could life be so cruel? I felt more scared than ever that day as I staggered to the bus stop a gibbering wreck. How could they justify this? One thing was sure. Your hold had been broken. Never, never, never would I step foot in that place again.

Never.

Visit 3

I told my parents I was going on a holiday; camping. It was late summer. I didn't care if they believed me. Didn't care if I arrived late. I didn't even care I'd agreed I'd never go back to that hell-hole again. 'You can go home at weekends,' they said. Was it a bribe? Who cares – it probably saved my life.

E2A, the best ward on the block. Everyone raved about it. Patients from other wards came to view, couldn't believe the pure luxury; a drinks machine, full-size pool table, your very own bedroom, and as for the Welsh dresser, it was a stunner. I remember the large windows; it was so sunny that light swooped in and was medication in itself. The rays lifted me up into their warm comforting arms and made me feel so good I was actually able to cry. I cried so hard that day. That hell-hole had become my haven. How could I ever hate what felt like the best home ever? I never wanted your hold to end. Even my emotions were beginning to return.

Visit 4

'I'm sorry Maddy, David committed suicide last night.' He was on lock up.

'Lucky bastard,' I said. How I regret my words.

Visit 5

Where had the sun gone? Why were the curtains drawn? Were the early-morning screams real or in my head?

Why couldn't this time be like the last time? Going out to the pub, being allowed to stay in bed late, having my nurse talk to me every day. Even the dresser looked smaller. No I won't be back. Hold or no hold.

Visit 6

I'd never been during winter before. It was a freezing, bitter late afternoon and as soon as my community nurse walked me through the doors again I thought, no. Not again. It's wrong. This time is different.

I only stayed one night. I actually discharged myself the next day. But hey, what about your hold on me? Was it at last lifted?

Visit 7

Wow. The Board Room. The grandest room ever where all the important people go. People so high up making executive decisions that I would never even begin to understand, let alone have an opinion on. Yet today, here I am. Me. Maddy the ex-inpatient actually disagreeing with nurses that I'd never dared make eye contact with, sharing views with professionals in mental health, representing other Service Users, fighting for them with managers of Cardiff and Vale NHS Trust.

Being given a chance to try to give a little back to all those people who helped me reach where I am today has been worth the hold Whitchurch has had on me. Only now when I walk along the corridors, I walk with pride, my head held high. I am a survivor of mental health. So thank you, Whitchurch. Long may your hold continue.

Maddy Read

What's inside the box?

I once heard of a famous writer who for whatever reason was locked away inside a mental institution for years on end. There was no hope of his release and it seemed he would spend the rest of his days there. One day a female writer, who was visiting the institution to give creative writing classes, recognised him from a picture in one of his books and initiated a conversation. Over a period of many visits they fell in love, he came back from the void, was released, and they lived happily ever after.

It was this tale I had fixed in my mind while en route to visit my stepfather in Whitchurch Hospital. He had paranoid schizophrenia, and had been sectioned for six weeks after not taking his medication. My mother had brought me along for emotional support, as her first visit to the hospital had left her feeling uneasy. The recovery chamber, so to speak, was on the second floor.

As we exited the stairwell and entered I immediately noticed a large pool table centre left of what was a very large sitting room. A man was standing there with a pool cue in his hand, repeatedly striking at a white ball which wasn't there; others were walking around in a daze, or staring at the floor whilst standing on the spot. Everyone seemed completely drugged up to the eyeballs, enough to allow them simply to go through the motions; totally glazed eyes, like some endless, mindless, drug-induced stupor; zombies.

My stepfather greeted us and led us to the smoking room. This room was completely yellow, and I would have thought it painted this colour had it not been for the circular swirls of off-white at shoulder level where someone had attempted in vain to wash the nicotine off. There were chairs against three of the walls, with one or two people chain smoking, looking at the floor. I was mindful of leaning back in the chair as I sat down, because the nicotine, which was also glistening with condensation, would have stained my clothes, and I knew it would have been a stain I would never, ever be able to remove.

It was a high-ceilinged room with a large window, very high indeed, locked of course. I took out my cigarette, lit up, and thought about my surroundings. This wasn't, or at least didn't seem to be, any place for recovery. And all previous impressions I had were fantasised or put there by Hollywood films. I thought about the story of the famous writer once more. Nobody was going to come and rescue *these* people. There would be no loving embraces, or loving guides to bring them back into the world.

That was it – there was no love. Not that I could point a finger at the staff, they were doing their job, and who would be able to work there day after day after day, and bring love into the place?

Visiting time was limited to the time of two cigarettes so it wasn't long before my mother and I said our goodbyes and left. Just outside the building was a well-tended lawn I had not noticed before. The wind was in the trees; if I blocked the building from my view it was the picture of serenity. Cars were going by, on the road just outside the main gate; people, most of them I would guess, oblivious to the secrets of this building. My mother asked me to get in the car and had to repeat herself. I realised then I had stood still too long. I had been smelling the air, as if for the first time.

Michael Oliver-Semenov

This moment

I am sat in a windowless room,
closed to everything outside,
closed to the architecture
and the garden's drizzling rain.

I am thinking about
how my father feels,
returning as a patient
after so long.

I am feeling tired and dreary,
wondering when
and from where
my next drink comes.

I am reflecting on my sister
in the secure unit,
coaxed by nurses
to take a bath.

But there is a window
in the bathroom door,
and three male patients
wandering by.

I'm claustrophobic,
disorientated,
with my back to the room
with the windows.

I want to go home.
I look up,
and I notice
there are skylights.

Anonymous

Living on the Edge 3

Jimmy suffers from Clinical Depression – Endogenous type. He wears his depression like a granite suit of armour, impervious now to contact with a world he has ceased to believe can offer him grace. His head and neck have long since disappeared into his shoulders, which over the years have stooped markedly. His feet scrape the floor as he walks. Lifting his feet has become too onerous. He never speaks, his expression never changes, his face is implacable. He sits in a chair at the edge of the room. Staff and patients repeatedly try to engage with him, but he is lost deep inside his granite chamber, unreachable. I never get to hear his voice.

And in my final weeks before leaving to return to university, as summer draws to a close, we organise a game of croquet outside on the lawn. Patients who were initially sceptical or too lacking in confidence to try something new, find themselves learning how to use the mallet to hit the ball through a hoop and to enjoy the experience.

On that day a group of humans left their psychiatric personas in the hospital and gathered on the lawn to enjoy the summer sun, to laugh together, to compete with each other, and to rest awhile in a space of sanity where their original personalities had a chance to shine through once more.

And in my late fifties, I enter the OT department room I once worked in, which is now a community physiotherapy department. The room looks worn out and uncared for. A new breed of professionals attend to the patients there now. They are young, agile, and helpful, an echo to me of my former guise there. I tell my therapist I used to work there. His response shows me he has no interest in me or my past. He has not lived long enough to understand the poignancy of my experience.

Now some fifty-five years since I lived at the edge of the hospital, I note that the politicians and decision-makers continue to parry about its future. Meanwhile the building, shabby and forlorn, offers scant inspiration for those who seek refuge there.

Where have those croquet players gone? Were they cured? Did care in the community really materialise for them? Only Carl remains as a visible answer to those questions. The doctors were right; they couldn't fix his life. He is looking older now and more frail. Sometimes I see him in Whitchurch village, one shoe and sock missing as he walks unaware of his chaotic grooming or the looks he attracts from the people around him. Other times I see him pacing the pavement outside the main entrance to the hospital, mumbling, focused on some internal dispute, hoping that this rhythmic movement will ease a resolution, the security of the hospital, as ever, close at hand.

Whitchurch Hospital has given me a window on humanity from a very young age. It has shown me the tragedy of human suffering, but also of the joy of recovery and healing. For one brief summer, my life collided with those of Carl and Irene, Tony, Jimmy, and Andy. Memories of those lives have touched me, informed me of what it is to be human, and remained in my thoughts to this day. Thanks to you all. I hope you each find peace of mind one day.

Ruth Hawkins

Rounds

There were at least half a dozen wards full of bed-ridden or semi-incapacitated elderly folk with dementia. A few unfortunate much younger souls with severe brain damage were among them. One man, in his thirties, had attempted suicide by gassing and was left in a 'vegetable' state. Such terminology was commonplace then. Over the months I worked there, the geriatric wards became full of ever more sick, incapacitated patients. Extra beds were put up in emergencies and rarely taken down again.

The over-stretched and under-trained nurses relied more and more on cot sides and medication for restraint and control. Basic washing, shaving, toilet care, and feeding were all that could be offered and sometimes not even that. Most of my time on those wards was spent listening to chests as the old dears coughed in my face. I had to organise blood tests, X-rays, antibiotics, and catheterisation, basic care which was eventually, and rightly, handed over to local GPs.

The gradual discharging of long-stay younger patients into the community had left empty beds. It seemed to make number-crunching sense to fill them with the dementing old people. I felt very sorry for the relatives I saw. Most Cardiffians, particularly the older generation, had a horror of 'ending up in Whitchurch', which still carried a stigma worse than the poor house. It seemed terrible that, because of a brain illness, they or their loved ones should have to do so.

My consultant was rather old-fashioned. He liked his juniors to visit each of his wards every morning and initial the ward notebook. I don't think most of his trainees had done this but I was always a suck-up, and anyway I quite approved of order and regulation. I would call into the two acute wards first and hope to get through all seven chronic wards by mid-morning, unless there was something urgent to detain me. I developed a loping walk, admirably suited to crossing the vast savannah of the hospital. I would barely pause in unlocking, going through, and relocking each door in a fluid movement, crossing the office to the desk in a few swift steps and signing my initials in the open ward book. My voice as I asked 'Any problems this morning?' must have barely registered before I was out again but the nurses grew used to the game and were able to stop me dead before I could escape, usually with such words as 'Could you look at Mrs Blank? She's chesty.'

One thing I definitely did not like was the cockroaches. The infestation of cockroaches was constant, though the numbers varied from a few busy specimens to a tidal wave of dozens. If you reported it you were not popular.

'We do NOT have cockroaches in the hospital!' I was firmly told.

'Oh, pardon my hallucinations then,' I was tempted to reply.

On my night rounds I would unlock the door at the end of each ward corridor. In the gloom I would detect a heaving sea of bodies. I hated the feeling of crunching them underfoot. No, let's rephrase that. I hated the feeling that I wanted to crunch them underfoot and would thoroughly enjoy the activity if I allowed myself to do so. A bit like treading on nice, crisp snow. Rather than face my nasty, inner cockroach-crusher, I took care always to turn the light on. I would pause for a moment and watch the surge, like the bow wave of a ship, towards the cracks under the skirting. Only then would I tread firmly and confidently along the corridor.

Elinor Kapp

The Whitchurch Hospital 'Campanile'

Whitchurch Hospital buildings include a tower. Constructed of rich red brick, with horizontal beige bands, it echoes the palette of the lower-rise hospital wings. It is crowned by a green copper dome, held aloft on a tier of small redbrick pillars, resting on an ivory-coloured cornice.

The tower, probably part of the hospital heating and ventilation system, acts as a landmark for miles around. We can see it from our first-floor living room bay window in Samuels Crescent. It can be glimpsed from Park Road, Velindre Road, and Heol Don. From Forest Farm it floats above the fields as if an Italian bell-tower – 'campanile' – had docked. Again by Radyr Weir along the Taff Trail a truncated version comes into view.

Unexpectedly, I saw it from the Number 24 bus where the North Road at Cathays crosses the railway line. It's perfectly on axis with the railway line at this point. Lastly, when walking in the hills north of Cardiff, I find the Whitchurch Hospital 'Campanile' calls once again.

Máire Kite

Whitchurch Hospital

In my early twenties, the most popular event held in Whitchurch Hospital was the New Year's Eve dance. It was well attended and there was no trouble whatsoever in the building, as patients weren't allowed to attend such functions.

However, on one occasion, before going to the dance, I was drinking at the bar of The Hollybush pub nearby to Whitchurch Hospital. I got into a conversation with a young person of roughly my own age and we got on well chatting about things in general.

Suddenly, out of the blue, he punched me hard in the stomach and ran out of the pub! I wasn't harmed very much, but the landlord of the pub, said 'That often happens here, he's one of the patients from the hospital over the road!'

Alun Williams

Slamming Ward Doors

SLAM! The empty room-ridden soulless sounds and echoes of wards around decrepit corridors. Bare, smelling of urine, tobacco, and vomit, along the institutional pale green walls.

Depraved wrecks of human existence puffing on their tiny remains of cigarettes, hands stained by nicotine, in dingy smoking rooms, walls stained and attempting to add to their few pence/week.

It is not their fault.

Diana Hodson

A Gormenghast Feel

I hadn't made a public appearance for some time. My brother had made his way through the unlocked door and found me in a foetal position, babbling nonsense and weeping, the room's surfaces scattered with bottles. The doctor was called, noted my Parkinsonion tremors and recommended I was taken off to the local hospital pronto.

Detox was short and brutal. After thirty-six hours, I was interviewed by a young, brusque duty shrink. He recommended a protracted stay in hospital for 'rest, recuperation, and therapy.' There was no doubt in my mind that I needed rest and recuperation and probably even therapy. With the booze drained from my system, my mind was a pandemonium of chattering demons, of terrors, guilt, and remorse. What I didn't want to do was stay in hospital. On the other hand, the outside world was full of snares: I knew for fact there was an unopened bottle in my flat. Finally, torn between my fear of hospitals and my fears of what my own behaviour might be like without the constraints of the institution, I agreed. He stood up, shook my sweaty, trembling hand in a business-like manner, and told me he'd arrange my transfer from detox to Ward A3C.

The hospital I was in was relatively modern and airy, painted in white and pastels. I dressed and packed my few toiletries. I hoped that A3C might indeed be a clean, well-lit, sanatorium-like place in which I might rest, recover some composure, and even regain some hope for the future.

I was sitting on my bed, waiting for the transfer up a floor, when the staff nurse clicked efficiently over and gave me an efficient smile.

'I just called your brother to tell him about your transfer. He seemed surprised that A3C was over at Whitchurch Hospital, and I thought I'd better tell you.'

If my brother was surprised, I was appalled. The blood drained from my head and if I wasn't sitting down I might have fallen over. Whitchurch was on the far side of the city. I'd visited a friend there who had cracked up twenty or more years ago. I still had vivid memories. It was vast, a crumbling Edwardian pile, a Dickensian workhouse turned psychiatric hospital, a place to which, in the minds of many, the old stigmas of the madhouse, the lunatic asylum continued to exist. I remembered the maze-like corridors, the snot-coloured walls, the slamming of doors, the occasional sight of a listless patient, and occasionally the faint cry of someone damned in the hell of their own delusions.

But I thought, despite my parched mouth and my heart trying to scrabble its way through my ribs, twenty odd years was a long time. Perhaps Ward A3C would indeed be a clean, well-lit place in which I could recover some composure and clarity of mind and regain some hope for the future; a hope I had lost along with my wife and children.

Whitchurch Hospital was the same great foreboding pile I remembered. Every inch the insane asylum for some Hammer Horror movie – crumbling brick, Gormenghast-like clock tower, Kafkaesquely missing the clock. The maze of corridors, now with flaked cream paint rather than the snot-coloured paint, but still the occasional listless patient shuffled by, and there was a distinct background bouquet of ugly institutional odours that seemed absent from the antiseptic corridors of my local hospital.

Structurally, A3C was not so daunting: dining area, pool table, two lounges with armchairs and sofas, televisions, and potted plants. Clearly some effort had been given to give it a non-institutional air. Still, I was reminded of an awkward hybrid of Fawlty Towers and Broadmoor. The bathing facilities were adequate. And best of all were the sleeping arrangements: individual bedrooms, tiny but clean and well-lit by day. I hoped to find some solace in my own private cubicle.

I was seen briefly by a sympathetic psychiatrist who went over my notes, and kindly but firmly suggested I stay in hospital for some while. The ward staff seemed equally sympathetic. The food was certainly better than at my local hospital. As a physical environment A3C was not so bad. What shocked me were the patients.

I'd expected my fellow inmates to be in similar states to myself, fucked up and in distress certainly, and in need of rest, respite, and possibly therapy but quickly I felt I had been plunged onto the set of *One Flew Over the Cuckoo's Nest*. The first patient to catch my attention was a middle-aged man with thin grey hair. His hands scrabbled constantly at nothing, his mouth lolled wide open, and when he did manage a semblance of speech it was either incomprehensible or delusional – he seemed to be complaining about non-existent black patches on his almost bare scalp. Inmates would shuffle past, faces blank masks, generally silent and unresponsive to greeting, zombified by drugs. They would slump into chairs, often drooling, stunned, and stare into space, eyes sometimes rolling wildly, or quickly fall asleep. The lounge televisions seemed to be always tuned to violent action movies.

One patient, Mark, a tall, obviously intelligent man of about my age approached me in a friendly manner as I paced up and down the corridor on my first night.

'So you're the new guy'

I assented.

'It's a madhouse in here,' he said and laughed.

I laughed too.

'Are you afraid?' he asked, eyes glancing up and down the corridor. 'You don't have to be.' He didn't sound convinced.

'No, I'm not afraid,' I answered, quite honestly. The notion of any kind of physical peril was far from my mind. What I did feel was quite torturous mental anguish. Not only was I racked with the anxiety of withdrawals, and remorse over my broken marriage and past behaviour, the disturbed nature of my fellow patients unsettled me greatly.

'I'm not really sick,' said Mark as we walked side by side up the corridor.

'I'm just a hypochondriac. I've read a lot of medical stuff so I can convince the quacks I've got anything. I shouldn't be here really.'

Excellent, I thought, someone else who doesn't feel they belong.

'Come and see this,' he said, motioning me towards his room.

Inside his room he showed me a very eloquent letter he had written to the Minister of Health, protesting the conditions of his hospitalisation. Wonderful, I thought, someone I can talk to. Then Mark began to bring out more and more copies of protest letters ranging from letters to the politicians at the local, national, and European Assemblies complaining about his status and treatment in hospital, to various letters to the hospital administration itself, complaining about the wastage of food on the ward. My smile felt more and more as if it was pinned on as I realised that Mark's problems went a little further than hypochondria. Luckily the call for nightly meds and lights out saved me. I curled up in my cubicle bed and, despite having been given a sleeping tablet, I waited through the night for the sky to get light again.

After twenty-four hours it had become clear I was going to find no rest or respite on A3C. The agitated and disturbed nature of most of the patients was exacerbating my own mental anguish. The mere mental strain of keeping the lid on my own hospital-induced anxieties prevented me from finding the composure and clarity of thought I had wanted from my time on the ward.

'Don't worry, you'll get used to life here,' said one male staff nurse solicitously.

'I really don't think so,' I quavered and, in truth, the idea of getting used to life the ward was not an idea I wanted to contemplate.

'Well, you can sign yourself out at any time against medical advice. You are a voluntary patient, all it takes is a signature from the duty doctor,' said a female staff nurse.

'OK,' I said, my resolve eroding.

'But,' she replied firmly. 'That would be AMA.' Her tone softened minutely. 'Why don't you wait until you see your own consultant and he can discharge you properly?'

I felt my resolve weaken further.

'All right,' I said. 'When will he be here?' I could hear the fear in my voice.

The nursing staff looked at one another doubtfully.

'He's promised to come by this evening after tea,' said one nurse without much confidence.

'Sevenish,' said another with a little conviction.

'OK,' I said, feeling this is as far as I could push this dispute without collapsing.

'Do you think,' I asked, 'I could get off the ward for a while now? I'd just stay in the grounds, get a bit of fresh air and exercise.'

The nurses looked at one another uncertainly then, the senior male nurse, as if tossing a hungry dog a bone, said,

'Yeah, just stay in the grounds.'

This, itself was a small, good thing, and I immediately changed into my shorts and sneakers and was away. I might have been a bit of a psychiatric snob but I was only a drunk with a touch of bipolar disorder – plus a whole caravan of actual personal problems – but I was not one of the groaners, droolers and general lunatics that made up the bulk of A3C'S population. I could still manage a rational conversation after all.

I spent a good four hours circumnavigating the hospital grounds before returning for tea. Oddly enough, my consultant finally did turn up as promised. I told him my reservations about the ward and its atmosphere was simply exacerbating my own condition.

'We-e-ell,' he said, sympathetically, 'It's not one of the more disturbed wards.' His eyes were worn, but showed an understanding of my distress.

'I understand,' I hastened to agree. 'But still in my case…'

'Look,' said the doctor. 'I suggest we give you a few more days to rest…'

'Rest!'

'Yes, rest. At least you are relatively free of physical needs…and the temptations you might experience outside. It's early days yet. You can't expect these things to swing back together too quickly. These things take time. Now I'll increase your tranquilizer dose slightly and we'll see you in another few days.'

'Er, OK,' I agreed.

I desperately wanted to leave but I wanted to do it the right way for the sake of my girls, whose welfare was my strongest lifeline against the void.

From then on, I stayed off the ward as much as possible. I spent many hours walking and jogging within the extensive grounds, not daring to stray to the nearby village. Just across the road from the hospital was a mini-mart with an extensive off-license shelf. It would have been so easy to stroll over, pick up a bottle, and be pissed in a few minutes. Still, I had no desire to take that easy stroll back to perdition – and anyway I avoided the temptation by keeping no money with me apart from a few coins for the phone or coffee machine.

And so I took up my routine of pacing, jogging, counting the rabbits, keeping to the margins, as far away from the hospital as possible.

After a day or two, I returned sweaty from my run and found the nurse's station unusually busy: phones were ringing constantly, even Clare, the very friendly, indefatigable manic, seemed barred. At tea time the more coherent patients were full of the subject.

'You won't be the new boy now,' said Jake to me, a boyish man with highly regrettable athlete's foot, giggling.

'I hear it's a real emergency case,' said Clare. 'The nurses are in a right state.'

Later that morning a thickset man with heavy gold earrings was wheeled in by his wife. He had a catheter bag that appeared not to be draining his bladder but abdomen. His eyes were half buried in his cropped skull. His skin was livid with a faint violet tinge and he looked very ill indeed but despite this he had the air of hard man about him.

He didn't emerge for breakfast, causing some speculation. But when I arrived back from my jaunt at lunchtime, there he was in his wheelchair. I was a little late so the only seat left was next to his.

'D'you mind if I…?' I began.

'No. Go ahead. He patted the chair. His voice was husky, but soft. 'Food's not bad.'

'A bit stodgy though, like they want to keep us well fed and quiet.' I introduced myself.

'Ray,' he grinned, shaking hands.

'Want a coffee or something?'

'Sure,' he said. 'A coffee would be nice.'

Anti-psychotics and other heavy meds tend to lead to naps so the lounge was almost empty. He wheeled himself over to a quiet sunny corner.

'Thanks,' he said, and I wondered again at the contrast

between his tough look and soft-spoken-ness. 'I never thought I'd end up in a place like this.'

'No,' I said.

'It's my own fault though...' he hesitated but he seemed as if he wanted to talk. 'I took some tablets...ended up on the poison ward...overdose.' He brought out the word reluctantly.

'Yeah,'

'I have had a lot of operations see...' He patted his upper abdomen.

'Twisted bowel and stuff...'

It seemed a valid enough reason, to think about ending it all, having your body carved up with no real hope of a successful outcome.

'I understand.'

Certainly it made more sense than the slow motion car wreck I had put my family and myself through and ended up here.

'I was over in the poison ward myself till they transferred me here,' I continued.

'How long have you been here?'

'Not long. Too long.'

He nodded and seemed about to speak when he was wheeled off by a nursing aide to change his dressings and catheter bag.

In the evening, Ray was already seated at the table with the groaning man and the scrabbling man. I nodded over at him but immediately after he was helped into his room, looking ill, and didn't emerge for Ovaltine and night time meds.

But at breakfast there he was out of his wheelchair, catheter bag still at his feet but looking more human. I waved him over to my table but the places were quickly taken by two of the permanently silent and John, whose vehement monologues seemed to moderate when he had his mouth full.

After breakfast, Ray was helped to his room again and I began my run. At lunch he didn't appear again. But the staff nurse told me my consultant would be here 'with luck' this evening. At last - a chance to get out with official approval. The first half of my jaunt was almost pleasant: the grass had just been mown and the air, unusually warm, was richly scented. After a time, I decided to pop back for a quick sluice on the ward. As I grabbed a towel from the linen closet, a staff nurse strolled over,

'I'm afraid your consultant has been called away,' she said brightly. 'He should be back the day after tomorrow.'

The sweat chilled on my skin.

'Oh.'

'Never mind. Just a day or two'

She might as well have said a decade or two.

The second half of my pre-dinner jaunt was less agreeable than the first: my demons returned in full force, with the warmth and sweet smell of new mown hay failing to distract me from their yammering.

Ray didn't return at dinner, but appeared at teatime and I made a point of sitting next to him.

'What's up Ray, where've you been?'

'In my room. Guts been playing me up. They get blocked.'

He held up a small carton and shook it. 'Then it's back to the milkshakes for a day or two.'

'That's a drag,' I said, guiltily tucking into my cottage pie.

Our tablemates, as was usual on the ward, bolted their food and were gone. We chatted for a while about inconsequential subjects as we drank our coffee. Then Ray leaned forward and lowered his voice,

'You know when they sent me here, I expected to meet people like you, people you could talk to. Maybe people with problems. But not,' he gestured around the ward at

59

the patients.

'I know what you mean,' I said.

'Look, taking too many tablets was stupid, I admit. And I admit I must have some problems to do something like that, what with my wife and my kid to think of. But not problems like these people.'

I nodded.

'When I came round on the poisons ward I was still woozy and the psychiatrist suggested they move me to place where I could recuperate. I knew I had problems so I agreed. Then they told me A3C was in Whitchurch. I tell you I broke down and had a little weep.'

I nodded again.

'I mean Whitchurch, it's still got that stigma doesn't it. I mean people think it's the loony bin don't they?'

'Yeah'

' I'm not a loony but I swear if I stay here much longer I will be.' His voice shook.

'I know what you mean. I have to get out of here as soon as I can before I go crazy. It's a madhouse in here,' I said, repeating Mark's joke.

'Not kidding. I mean the way that some of the patients talk and act it's enough to do your head in…Hang on a minute.' John and Mark walked past. 'I don't want cause any more friction. Listen, why don't we get together and have a quiet chat sometime.'

'Great,' I said, thinking at last a patient I can talk to.

Ray's wife and daughter arrived then and I left them to a family visit.

The next day Ray didn't emerge from his room and I spent it pacing and jogging as usual. But the following day Ray was there for breakfast and we made plans to meet at the hospital bowling green after lunch. Ray disappeared into his room and I was about to change into my shorts when a staff nurse came to tell me that my consultant was expected on the ward that morning and could I wait on his arrival. I most definitely could. I went straight to my room and packed my clothes determined this time to be discharged. Miraculously the doctor actually arrived on time.

Again I argued that the conditions on the ward were simply worsening my anguish, that my confinement with much more seriously disturbed patients in my fragile state was not a good idea.

'What about the world outside?' he asked. 'How will you cope?'

'I don't know but I know I can't cope here. Look I'm willing to do any outpatient therapy, see anyone, get any help you want, as long as I can get out.'

'You can leave any time, you were a voluntary patient,' He said with a wry smile.

'I know. But I wanted to leave in the right way.'

'Very well, I'll see you at outpatients next week. Good luck.'

And off he went to sign the papers. I couldn't believe it.

I called my brother, told him I was discharged and he said he'd be there within the hour. When I came back from pharmacy with a week's worth of medication I called by Ray's room but it was empty. Then my brother was there. I embraced him.

'What's up broth?' I said.

'Happy to get out?' he grinned.

'Damn straight. Let's go.'

As we walked towards the car park, I glanced back at the bowling green, and there hunched over in the slight drizzle was Ray. I was tempted to walk over and say goodbye or even just yell out,

'I'm off! Good luck!'

But somehow I couldn't bring myself to do it. I got in the car and turned round to watch Ray recede through the rain bleared windows.

'A mate of yours?' asked my brother.

'No not really. It's not a place you make mates exactly.'

I turned to the front. The windshield wiped the beads of rain off the window.

Russell Taylor

Working at Whitchurch

One of the night staff going on duty accompanied me up the endless drive to the Hospital's main building. She introduced herself as Staff Nurse Delgado and she directed me to the matron's office – reminding me to replace my hat before knocking on the door.

Miss Mowbray was not the dragon I expected. She asked a nurse to show me to my room, located in the Male Home, where I was able to wash and brush up. I was then taken to the nurses' common room. Two nurses had just come off duty, still dressed in their uniforms of blue- and white-striped cotton dress, white cotton apron, and white starched cap, and taking me under their wing, they suggested that we go for a drink in the Hollybush Inn along the road. I had never been in a pub before, except when we visited Auntie Amy in Oakengates and even then not for a drink. Afraid of being thought unsociable I agreed to go with them and had a glass of cider, which cost about seven pence. From then we went for a walk along by the railway before returning to the hospital, our rooms, and bed.

After breakfast I was issued with the Preliminary Training School Uniform – white coat, striped cotton belt, and white cap – and directed to the Nurse Training School where I met my fellow probationers. The sister tutor was Miss Mary O'Shaughnessy, a lady dressed in a grey uniform with white collar and a nun-like triangular cap which covered most of her hair.

In school, we took notes from dictation by Miss O'Shaughnessy. I remember one *faux pas* by someone who had written down 'send for lemonade' when Miss. O'S. had said 'send for medical aid' and another when 'explosion of faeces' was written for 'expulsion of faeces'. We listened and took notes from lectures given by the medical staff, one of whom was our heart-throb, Dr Spillane. We remained in school for about three months before taking up our duties on a ward of our own choice.

Our working hours were 'split shifts' when I first started, but shortly afterwards were restructured to from 7.30 a.m. until 7.30 p.m. with quarter of an hour for morning break, three quarters of an hour for lunch, and half an hour for afternoon tea for four days. Then it was 7.30 a.m. until 1 p.m. for one day. That meant that we had two and a half days off duty and worked a total of 47.5 hours per week.

The nurses' table for writing reports was at the head of the dormitory in front of a coal fire, which was set and lit by the nursing staff. The dayroom was large and airy with seats in the windows which looked out over the airing courts – a fenced area of grass with a few trees and shrubs – in which the patients were able to take some exercise under supervision.

All the wards were locked in those days and the nursing staff were issued with keys that we had to carry on a chain attached to our pockets, and which fitted the various doors within the hospital wards. Whitchurch was considered to be one of the foremost mental hospitals in the country, and we prided ourselves that we never used the 'pads' (padded cells) other than to store clothing and other ward equipment. One day I went to look for something in the pads and was inadvertently shut in. It was not for more than a few moments before I was missed and the door opened, but the feeling of claustrophobia was quite overwhelming, and I feel that although sane I would have gone mad if left in there for long. For the same reason I never knew the strait-jacket used, though we were allowed to use a fair amount of manual restraint when and if necessary.

'Treatments' were few and far between as psychiatry was still very much in its infancy. We did have hydrotherapy which could be as simple as a warm bath, or a needle spray that sprayed warm water over a patient's body in an effort to calm her down. I had to sit in with a patient one day. She was put in a warm bath, but because she was so disturbed she had to be tied into the bath with a sort of canvas blanket. The water was kept at an even temperature all day but even so she kept on pleading with me to release her. Despite all my denials and reassurances she was convinced that eventually we would let her drown.

Patients were given a dose of 'opening medicine' or 'jollop' each week whether needed or not. There was a saying that the height of luxury was to be constipated in a mental hospital! A queue of patients would form first thing in the morning – usually Monday – the ward sister having prepared a table with bottles of every known substance necessary to open the bowels. All patients were observed and charts were duly marked with 'B.O.' (Bowels Open) or 'P.U.' (Passes Urine) each day. A 'B.N.O.' on the chart was considered almost as serious as 'P.N.U.'!

One of the most interesting treatments was known as Insulin Shock Therapy and this was carried out in a small specially adapted unit off one of the wards. Treatment was usually started off in the patient's 'home' ward and entailed a small dose of insulin being administered each morning after an overnight fast. No food or drink was allowed for an hour or two. The dose of insulin was slightly increased each day, until the patient showed signs of 'sopor'. This is a condition in which the patient does not respond intelligibly to speech, but responds to reflex stimulation. On reaching this stage the patient was transferred each morning to the Special Unit where stronger doses of insulin were administered until a full state of coma was reached. The first coma suffered was reversed after fifteen minutes by the induction of glucose either by intubating directly into the stomach, or by intravenous injection. Subsequent comas were gradually increased to last for about an hour. I remember one patient who remained in a coma for longer. It had become 'irreversible' and the doctor and the rest of us worked like Trojans, pumping in glucose and Vitamin B1. We were more than relieved when she eventually came round.

We had many cases of tuberculosis, and when I was on night duty on F2 ward which was the infirmary ward, there was a young woman who was suffering from a T.B. lesion in the brain. She was very sick as a result – both mentally and physically – and from the time I went on duty and all night she screamed 'Give me something to make me sl-e-e-p'. She had been given all her prescribed medication so I was unable to help her other than to try and soothe her. Treatment by antibiotics was still very new but it was decided to try the new drug Streptomycin on her. It was a miracle. Emily turned from a maniac into a lovely young woman who helped us in the ward as soon as she was well enough.

A patient brought in by the police from somewhere near Cardigan was a tiny waif of a creature in her early twenties. She could speak hardly any English as Welsh was her first language and just kept on repeating 'Want to go 'ome'. Apparently she'd had a little baby and had put it on the fire, and of course the child had died. My friends and I thought that probably she had been cold in the primitive conditions in which many rural people still lived and, being what was then known as 'mentally subnormal', she wanted to warm the baby. I don't know what became of her but I do hope that the law was lenient with her.

Of course, we nurses had to lay out any patient who had died and it could be quite frightening when the residual air in the lungs was expelled in a groan and the patient appeared to be still alive. We were required to make the body suitable to the family in order to make death as tolerable as possible.

After washing the remains, we stuffed the nose and other orifices of the body with clean cotton wool, combed the hair and pared the nails, shaved male patients when required, and put pennies over the eyes to keep them closed. A crepe bandage was used to support the chin, making sure that dentures did not pull the face out of shape. The finishing touch was to tie a label with the name of the patient, ward, and date of death onto the big toe. The body was then wrapped in a clean white sheet and left on the screened bed ready to be taken to the mortuary.

Evelyn Evans

Footsteps

I worked on the hospital in the 1960s. I was working for a contractor and we were building an extension.

Our bricklayer, he'd never go down in the ducts on his own. By ducts I mean big passageways below the hospital. They took electricity cables, drains, and things. Their purpose was so that you didn't have to dig up the floors if there was a problem.

Anyway, this brickie, he'd be terrified if he had to go down there. You could hear every footstep above your head and it sounded like someone was right behind you – creeping up on you, like. You'd swear there was someone there, behind you in the darkness. I used to have to go down with the bricklayer and sit with him as he did his work. So I know it's true; it was a trick with the sound. And it was, quite simply, frightening.

We had a Portakabin in the grounds. The patients used to wander in. One of them, he loved crusts. He'd been in Hensol and there they left the crusts on the sandwiches. Not at Whitchurch, they cut them off. He'd come to us and we'd give him our crusts. We'd leave them for him if we were away. He loved his crusts.

Ivor Betty

Perceptions of Whitchurch Hospital

The hospital was to me like the hotel in *The Shining*. To me a timeless palace. I have a myriad of images, thoughts, impressions, sensations in my mind of Whitchurch Hospital. As well as lots of tea and fags. Endless beauty and horror. Extremely scary and others scared. Epic tapestry, evolving, convoluted, twisted, spacious, holy, fragmented. Everything was significant, from a cigarette butt in the ashtray to the entire universe. Intense, mind-rippingly intense.

One beautiful memory on a clear, bright day: padding barefoot on pebbles with James, another 'client,' just outside a door from a corridor. In my mind I was paddling in a cool stream with this lovely person.

Lying on my bed in the day listening to the music of Faithless on headphones. A cassette given to me by an adorable man who invented perpetual motion, and called me Sharky as I referred to sharks often and liked them. Every sound resonated in my mind.

I deeply loved the 90s. All about baseball, rock, grunge. An exotic and sensitive soul taught me to handle a basketball in the gym. Made me feel like I was experiencing the spirit of this era. Unfortunately things had become horrific in my mind. I thought all the terrors of hell were to be unleashed on my body and soul. I slit my wrists at home.

A friendship bracelet my sister had made me, orange, yellow, and white thread were stained in blood. I believed my sister was actually a witch and I had only just realised. Terrified, I thought it was important to take off the bracelet. This basketball angel took me over to her room where it was warmly lit and had a powerful warming atmosphere. On the table was a vertical white little branch, she said if you want you can hang the bracelet on it. Which I did. She kept it for me. After time, don't know how much time went by – days, weeks, who knows. I asked for it back, it was still on the little tree, as I think of it and I wore it again. I realized my beloved sister was only my sister and not a witch.

At home, while becoming more out of touch with everyday reality and entering another world, I believed I could communicate with and heal cats.

A memory that starts with me sitting on a comfortable chair in a hall on the hospital blue carpets, I think, a table with flowers and warm lighting, daytime. I must have recently been admitted to hospital. Two young nurses introduced themselves and asked me questions about myself. I remember they were so friendly.

They asked 'Why do you think you are here?' and I said smiling and slightly laughing, 'I think I can help cats.' I don't know why I laughed, because I believed I really could. And they both laughed affectionately.

Peace and sanctuary from the madness of world. Occupied by the most interesting and fascinating people in the world. My spiritual home.

When I arrived, though, I thought I entered the realm of hell. A nurse was putting on a green plastic apron. I thought I was to be eaten alive. I slowly and fearfully walked into the main TV room and knelt down in middle of the room, waiting for an attack from the demons (patients as I later discovered) that thankfully never came. A demon/patient licked his teeth. I was absolutely terrified.

The building was a beautiful building full of character. I loved it, I still do, and I believe to this day it loved me too. I draw parallels with my feelings with Whitchurch

Hospital to *The Shining*. I wouldn't like to go back now because you can't; I'm a different person. I have recovered a great deal. But the hospital will always haunt my memories. It is a building with a SOUL.

Rattling of the tea trolley, distant footsteps and voices, silence, atmospheres, dreamy and creamy, heaven and hell, HOME, warmth, darkness and light, smoky, trapped, and safe.

Anonymous

Visiting My Aunty

I was feeling very excited. I was allowed to go and visit my Aunty Mary in Whitchurch Hospital. Before, my parents did not think I was old enough to visit her by myself, but at the age of thirteen, they said I could go.

I'd missed seeing my aunty whilst she was in hospital, as she was my favourite relative on both sides of the family. She was very special and she doted on me and my sister. We even shared our second name – Elizabeth. My aunty usually lived at home with her mother, my nana, and we would regularly go down and visit them. I missed my aunty when she had her 'funny turns' and need to go to hospital. I longed to visit her there. It was only later when I was seventeen or eighteen that I realised my aunty had Schizophrenia.

I wondered at the time why people would refer to the hospital as the 'mad house.' I knew my aunty was admitted there several times over the years and my aunty was not mad, she was the nicest and kindest person I knew.

I remember catching the Whitchurch bus and I asked the driver to tell me where to get off. I then got off the bus and walked through the gateway and along the path. I asked where her ward was, one of the west wards. The man gave me the directions.

I remember walking down long corridors that seemed never ending. On the way down the corridors I saw people: some were in pairs and some were alone. They were all talking, some to themselves. There was a background noise of chatter where you could hear noise, but not the words.

After what seemed like an eternity I eventually got to the ward. I opened a door and was faced by a block of stairs. I walked up those stairs to a front door. On the door was a sign saying 'Could all visitors report to the ward office before seeing their relatives.' I walked down a short corridor and came to a dayroom. It was very large and around the perimeter were easy chairs, in which people sat. The whole room was very smoky and most of the people sitting were smoking. I went to the ward office and asked if I could see my aunty. They said yes and then I saw her, sitting in a chair, smoking and staring into space. I went over to see her, when she saw me she smiled while puffing on her cigarette. Her finger was stained yellowy brown.

We sat and talked for a while then a member of staff came over and said to my aunty, 'Why don't you take your niece to the café?' We then left the ward. I remember that my aunty was more animated and talkative in the café, She seemed like her normal self.

We finished our tea and she took me on a tour of the hospital. We went to the shop. She bought more cigarettes and some sweets for me. We then walked back to the ward. While there I had to speak to the staff about my aunty's condition for my parents. I looked around the ward to see if I could see any members of staff but I could not see anyone in uniform and I wondered who was looking after the patients if there were no nurses around. My aunty looked at me and pointed to a lady wearing a red blouse and black skirt. She said that was the nurse. I was so surprised as when I visited my nana in the Heath the nurses wore uniforms. So I went to the nurse and asked how my aunty was. Then, being the inquisitive thirteen-year-old girl that I was, I asked her why she was not wearing a uniform and she said that in psychiatric hospitals they did not wear any uniforms.

I went back to my aunty thinking to myself, what are

psychiatric hospitals and why are they different from normal hospitals? It was a few years before I realised what they were and what they treated.

Tracy Hartwell

History Snapshot – 2

The first report or enquiry into the state of provision for what were called 'criminal and pauper lunatics' in England and Wales took place as early as 1808.

What emerged was a picture of poor basic care in both the private and public hospitals. In nearly all of the establishments inspected there was terrible overcrowding, lack of decent sanitation, and clear evidence of fairly barbaric treatments such as bleeding, cold baths, and purging.

Although the report led to the passing of the Asylums Act, there was no compulsion for local authorities to create such provision and by 1845 only eighteen counties had built hospitals for people with mental health problems.

The new Asylums Act of 1845 changed all that, making the provision of county asylums compulsory. The second half of the century duly saw the development of a system or network of asylums right across Britain. They were enormous institutions, the Victorians quickly realising that this was not just compliance with legislation, it was also a way to make money.

Not every local authority was in a position to build an asylum, at least not in the short term. And many were forced to 'buy in' places from other authorities until such time as they were financially able to create their own establishments.

At the beginning of the nineteenth century Cardiff was still a small town, boasting a population of well under 2000. However, with its rapid growth as a port for the export of Rhondda coal, as the century unfolded the town witnessed an enormous population explosion. By 1871 there were over 39,000 people living grouped around the docks – by 1900 that figure had increased to over 150,000. It was inevitable that mental health problems would become a significant factor.

The county of Glamorgan, in compliance with the 1845 Asylums Act, had created a hospital for people with mental health problems at Bridgend, the first patients being admitted in 1864. Originally intended for just 300 patients, it was quickly found to be too small and in 1880 the establishment was extended.

An agreed number of mental health patients from Cardiff had been admitted to the Bridgend asylum since 1865, the places being paid for out of the town's Poor Rate. By the last year of the century there were 476 Cardiff patients in what was, by now, a grossly overcrowded and one might say dangerous county asylum. This figure of 476 was thirty more than the agreed number.

It was not just the county asylum at Bridgend that took Cardiff patients. Nearly 700 more were placed in asylums at places such as Carmarthen and Chester. Clearly there was an urgent need for Cardiff – now the premier town in Wales – to provide its own asylum.

In 1905 Cardiff became a city. And now it was not just a matter of providing care and help for a very needy section of society – now civic pride and dignity demanded that Cardiff should be able to provide all the social, medical, and cultural amenities that its new-found status demanded. And that included a city asylum.

Phil Carradice
Author, historian and lead writer on The Whitchurch Project

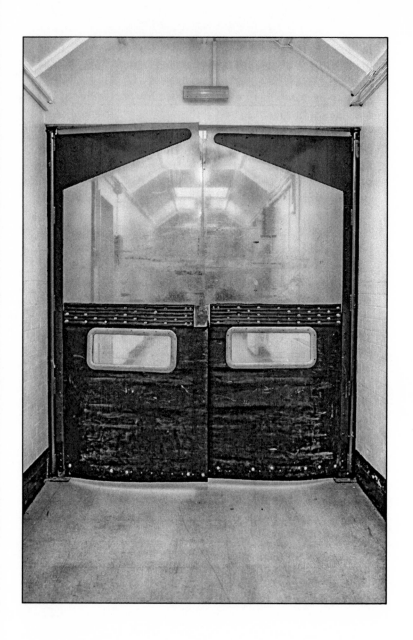

Colours

I love my pastel rainbow jumper
its soft changing colours
can always lift my mood

But here for the staff
it's a sign of mania
– they watch me like a hawk
maybe even increase the sedation

I soon discover
to survive in this strange place
dark, sombre colours are best
look dull and dreary
if you want to be released.

Marilyn Kemeny

Intensive Care Unit

Someone rang the doorbell.
Someone answered.
I was ushered in.
Nowhere to hide.
Nowhere to cling.
Desperation's aspirin
Nowhere to be found.

I stared at the ground.
Years of sad soles
Had worn their way
Into the carpetless floor
As they made the passage
Through their rage.

The smell of institutional food
Lingered in my nostrils
Sending messages of past moods
To my brain.

I had been here before
My story repeats itself
Again and Again.

The rain on the windows
Began to beat down.
The clown in me
Began to fade.

The high sash windows
Made to open
One inch
Kept us frightened animals
In our pen.

A copper beech tree
Looked majestically on me
And my sorrow.
And made me believe
In tomorrow.

Anonymous

Memories of one of the daughters of the hospital superintendent

My father, Dr Thomas John Hennelly, was appointed Medical Superintendent in 1937 at the early age of thirty-two (and at a starting salary of £1,000 per annum!)

I was born, the fourth of five children, in a large lovely house in extensive grounds of about three acres comprising a wood in which we had our very own 'Magic Faraway Tree', another wood of just hazelnut trees, a grass tennis court, rose garden, vegetable garden, chicken run, and extensive lawns. The house, called Velindre, was built for the sole purpose as accommodation for the incumbent physician superintendent of the hospital. It only stopped being used for that purpose when my father left in 1960 as his successor already had a house in Whitchurch and felt no need to move. As the hospital opened in 1907 I believe, presumably the house was built at the same time, alongside the hospital grounds. My father's journey to work was about a five-minute walk.

During the war the hospital was taken over by the military and used for recuperating wounded prisoners of war. My father became an honorary major. I was too young to remember any of that but I did end up with an American godfather.

Our house was connected to the hospital by internal telephones, of which there were three in the house – one by my father's bed, one in his study, and one in the hall. You can imagine the fun we had as it was like having very sophisticated walkie-talkies to talk to each other on. Needless to say we never played with these phones when my father was at home!

Our 'outside' phone number was Whitchurch 4. My mother was the local GP in Whitchurch and patients would phone our house if they wanted a visit from her. I distinctly remember taking a call from a patient when my mother was out, asking for her to visit, and forgetting to take down ANY details of the patient's address or phone number or even their name. You can imagine her anger when I had the courage to admit to what I had or rather, hadn't done! I am convinced my phobia of the telephone is as a result of that episode.

We had a wonderful childhood. We would wander over to the hospital farm where we made camps in the haystacks, played with piglets, even rode a cow. We seemed to be allowed to just roam free. There were tennis courts in the hospital grounds where we spent hours playing tennis. We watched the cricket matches and bowling on the beautifully manicured green between the front of the hospital and the chapel. Each year there was a sports day for the patients which we always went to. As Dr Hennelly's children we were treated as royalty. The downside of this, of course, was that we always had to be on our very best behaviour!

There were regular evenings of entertainment in the hospital – we frequently attended film nights sitting in the front row and I clearly remember patients coming up to us and giving us little bags of sweets they had bought in the hospital shop. Again at the annual Christmas show we were in the front alongside my father, mother, and several important dignitaries.

Every Christmas Day the matron, nursing, and medical staff would walk over to our house for drinks. My father would spend hours on the wards on Christmas Day and we would join him for some of it. Then on Christmas night my parents always threw a party for friends and family. Somehow, as well as all this, they managed to give us five children a lovely Christmas Day.

A number of the patients used to come over to our house daily and work for us. Ellen, who was as round as she was tall, would cook for us. She was a manic-depressive, so would 'disappear' for days, presumably when she wasn't well. She was like one of the family really and certainly for her we were the closest she had to a family of her own. I clearly remember after my brother was diagnosed with diabetes when he was thirteen, Ellen very carefully measuring out the exact carbohydrates and making John's 'special fairy cakes'. Awen, I can't really remember what she did – cleaning I think. My brother remembers her as being paranoid schizophrenic. I just remember she wasn't loveable like Ellen and I would sometimes be on the receiving end of her sharp tongue. Edward, or 'Tedward' as I, as a three/four-year-old called him, did odd jobs around the place. He apparently worshipped me, and would do anything I asked of him, even to the point of shutting himself in the chicken pen all day because I 'ordered' him to do so and staying there obediently until someone noticed he was missing and came to find him! Sounds dreadful, doesn't it?

Each week in the summer an army of men from the hospital would arrive, many on sit-on lawn mowers, to tend to the gardens, which always looked immaculate.

My sister had bad asthma as a child and spent many an hour with the hospital physiotherapists, who gave her various exercises. If any of us injured ourselves we were taken over to the hospital for an X-ray. I have a clear picture of walking through the hospital orchard to the hospital with my mother who had managed to 'sew' her finger or thumb with the electric sewing machine, pouring blood into a terry-towelling nappy wrapped around it. I guess one of the many doctors in the hospital, who were all our friends, dealt with the injury.

The occupational therapy department made us a dolls'

house which was an exact replica of our house – I would love to know what happened to it.

I have newspaper cuttings from when my father left Whitchurch to take up a specialist psychiatric post in Canada. They talk about him being 'a pioneer', doing away with the padded rooms, introducing an open-door policy in the hospital, creating a day hospital where non-resident patients could get treatment, and introducing group psychotherapy to Whitchurch. My memories are of a happy childhood where we spent many an hour in the hospital among 'friends' who lived there and we were all cared for – I don't remember ever being fearful – I accepted the patients' behaviour as 'different' but rarely questioned it.

Angela Sadler (née Hennelly)

Memories from one of the sons of the hospital superintendent

I think it was in 1958 or 1959 that some government official or other decided that mental patients whose occupational therapy was to work in doctors' households were phased out of such employment because it was considered that such work was demanding. Or some such thing.

My father was Chief Medical Superintendent of Cardiff City Mental Hospital from 1937 to 1960. I was his youngest child. I had the run of the place – the hospital, a 106-acre farm, orchards, playing fields, and a house on a three-acre estate.

We had a household of staff comprising of patients. There was Ellen, a manic depressive, who cooked. Awen, paranoid and schizophrenic, was the maid. Edward was the manservant. I think he was simple minded. And of course Simon, who hadn't got out of bed until he was forty, was the gardener. He never complained if I was rude or misbehaved, but Awen became violent if I or my sister teased her about her madness. Children can be cruel. We were no exception. In fact, the only time my mother ever slapped me was because I was rude to Awen. It was a sharp hard smack across the back of my leg. It hurt like hell, and I've never been rude to anyone ever since.

The patients were my friends. They were normal as far as I knew what that meant. Occasionally I detected behaviour that seemed different from what my parents were teaching me was expected. Behaviour I later learned made it difficult for them to live in the real world. The hospital was a safe haven. None of the patients I knew ran away.

When our staff had to quit they were phased out. From working full time they were reduced to twice a week, then once a week, then finally, not at all. I watched Ellen, Awen, Edward, and Simon sink into their respective madnesses as it dawned on them that they had no control over their own lives. Simon grew introverted, as did Edward. Awen became severely paranoid and eventually lost herself in her schizoid reality. And Ellen waxed steadily more manic then more depressed. She died within the year.

Losing these people, who were my earliest friends, was my first experience of loss.

Dermot Hennelly

Visiting

When we first moved to Whitchurch a lot of people asked if we were worried about the close proximity to the hospital. We weren't very concerned but we were very careful, walking along the pavement opposite the hospital because a few of the patients used to sit or lean on the walls there and, in our ignorance, we were a little afraid of them. Little did I know that I would become a regular visitor to the hospital when my mother was admitted there twelve years later.

I first entered the hospital through the main porch to ask where I could find the ward my mother was on. The overriding impression was of neverending corridors – bleak, overwhelming, with thoughts of workhouse Victoriana going through my mind. When you eventually came to the door that led to the ward you were faced with equally imposing stairs that eventually stopped at a locked door. When this door opened we entered a separate world operating with its own rules and routines, where the sick and despairing were cared for and protected from themselves. The staff were cheerful and the more that you entered this world the more accustomed you became to it. We would be sat with my mother and it wasn't unusual for the man – a teacher – opposite to rise from the sofa and execute somersaults across the room. As time went by we became used to this sort of behaviour. We would chat to the other patients while our children played on the pool table with some of the younger people.

The grounds of the hospital seemed appealing and attractive. I have memories of running around them as a child, during an earlier stay by my mother, many years before. I took a little potted cactus to the hospital to show my mother and somehow lost it in the grounds – I thought that at least it might grow in this garden!

A number of people are very interested in the history of the farming activity that was undertaken at the hospital. The days of hospital self-sufficiency are now long gone but what a brilliant thing in its day. The hospital is a landmark building and we can locate the area by spotting the tower from as far afield as my brother's home in Penarth.

Sue Vanstone

Curls

The phone rings and I twirl down the stairs in my mother's petticoat and my silver party shoes. The latter bought with a tantrum that means I must alternate wellies and smelly black rubbery plimsolls to school for a whole term. A small price to pay. 'Hello,' I trill down the phone.

'Hello, Emma, it's me, Lucy.'

Lucy. My foster sister, a sporadic inhabitant of my little-girl world. When I was really little (I am a big girl, nearly eight now), I would curl onto her lap and hold my gubby up to her face to catch the delicious cigarette smoke for later. My gubby, a bedraggled remnant of candy-striped cot sheet, was hooked between my fingers. I would laboriously crook index and ring finger into my mouth, thumb stroking my cheek, little finger against my nose, and inhale the collected scents of Players No. 6 and Marmite.

Her appearances are more intermittent since we moved to Wales. She is busy being in places called Borstal and Holloway. Now she is in a hospital called Whitchurch, getting the drugs out. We have visited her. She and the others were working on a big, brightly coloured picture with lots of felt pens. It is crazed with different patterns. Psychedelic. I hug this word. I can spell it. And Czechoslovakia. And Turquoise. Before she went to hospital I remember disturbed nights. Blue lights flashing across my bedroom wall. Dinner parties disrupted.

'Is your mum there?'

'Mummy and Daddy have gone to the theatre; Mrs Cook is looking after us. She's going to make my hair curly.'

'Oh. I just rang to say goodbye'. Her voice is thick and slow. Funny.

'Oh, Lucy, you are silly. You don't ring up to say goodbye. You ring up to say hello'. And I spin off to wriggle as our elderly babysitter helps me fulfil my fantasy of tumbling golden tresses. I have known for some time that I am a fairy princess, stolen by gypsies and given to my parents. My limp curtains of poker-straight hair do not match my idea of how I should really look. It will be coiled up in rags and I will sleep, carefully keeping my head off the pillow, for a fretful night. In the morning everyone will see me for what I really am. Tar, la, la. The most beautiful girl in the world.

In the morning, when the rags are removed, my hair is indeed curly. I shake it, practise tossing my head haughtily as princesses do. The curls crash to my shoulders, vanish, leaving kinky, badly ironed curtains, tucked behind wing-nut ears.

By the morning Lucy's body has been found in the hospital grounds; the fistfuls of hoarded barbiturates too efficient for another phone call.

Emma Geliot

Pain Through Walls

Whitchurch? A sad place, walking zombies in the corridors. So depressing, in a way. It was mainly the corridors – all those men, just walking. It was so sad, for so many of them. This place was their home, they'd been there for years. And all they did was walk.

One of my most striking memories remains doing ECTs for chronically depressed patients. You would see their bodies shaking with the electric current – I felt as if it was going through my heart. I wanted to hug them, say it was all going to be all right. But you couldn't, not openly. You had to stay distant, stay professional.

The corridors? When you see a horror film you sometimes hear a sound, a noise, a whooshing noise. That's what the corridors sounded like with the wind blowing, people walking, doors opening and closing. The echoes – terrible.

At times you could feel and hear the pain through the walls. People have walked there, lived there, and it's as if they've left something – some part of them – behind.

At night it's quite frightening. At night you feel as if someone is walking behind you – all the time. Those corridors, the memories of those corridors, stay with me all the time. In winter in particular.

The long nights weren't nice. Perhaps in summer, with bright sunshine, the place wasn't too bad. But in winter? Very depressing. All those long gloomy nights. And then the madness comes. It hits you like a hammer. And that's just the staff. God knows what it does to the patients.

Lata

It Could Have Been Me

I have only been to Whitchurch Hospital three times. The first time I went there was to visit a friend. That day is ingrained on my mind and just as real to me as it was on that September day almost twenty years ago.

One day, a year or so later, her son turned up on my doorstep. He was living with foster parents. His mother was 'in Whitchurch'.

I went one glorious sunny Saturday afternoon in September. My intention was to say hello, see how she was, if she needed anything, then go. That's not quite how it worked out. I found my way to the ward, no mean achievement. The hospital was clearly constructed during Victorian times and had many staircases in strange places. I remember going through a door in a wall on the side of a corridor, then winding up this enclosed staircase, which seemed more suited to a church tower than as an entrance to a ward. When I arrived on the ward, I was surprised to see that it was so huge. I enquired about my friend and was asked various questions before I was allowed to go to see her. I was shown through the large general ward area to some individual units at the far end of the ward. These units were clearly of a later construction, containing large windows looking down the ward, the remainder was painted white. The paintwork had the appearance of wood which had had many years of paint, layer upon layer of it.

Initially I was shocked. She was so emaciated. She was a tall woman and yet she weighed about six stone. On one side she was visibly battered and bruised, she told me that she had been trying to do her ironing, but had been too

93

weak to manage it and had fallen over the board. I didn't doubt this for a second. She was very happy and friendly, but I felt that she didn't know who I was, her manner was childlike. She told me that it had been her birthday the previous day, pointing to her cards, but was too weak to stand to show them to me. She spoke in a very childlike manner, she could have been a two-year-old. I had taken her photographs of our children from a day trip we had made. This made her excited, gleeful even. She asked me to brush her hair. I did, for quite some time. It was long, thick, and quite knotted. I feared that she would never recover and that this absence she seemed to be experiencing was some sort of dementia. Such a bubbly outgoing, vivacious young woman, who had lost her children, her sanity, her life!

I found it very tough, but smiled and talked to her all afternoon. Then came the time when I had to go. I hugged her and fought back the tears, told her that I would visit her boys, then left her room. As I passed the adjacent unit I stopped to look in, it was empty. I stood for a while looking at the empty bed. It was all too clear to me that it could have so very easily been mine.

In the years since that day, when depression has loomed over my life, through infidelity, marriage breakdown, debt, divorce, and many other horrors, no matter how bad I have been, that single thought is what has given me the tenacity to carry on going, to keep sane. That could have been me.

Gillian Collins

Baby

When my son was a year old I went to my GP and she wanted to admit me to hospital, but I did not want to leave my son. My GP tried to admit me to the mother and baby unit in Sully but at a year old he was too old to be admitted. So my GP said I could either go in voluntarily or she would section me.

So I went to Whitchurch voluntarily. I arrived on the ward feeling very low and in great despair, I was missing my son immensely. I remember patients and staff sitting around in the dayroom. One nurse showed me to my bed and I put my clothes away. I then went and sat in the chair and just looked out of the window, seeing nothing, just thinking about my son. I sat in the chair till about ten o'clock when I could no longer cope. I rang my house where my sister was looking after my son. I cried down the phone and pleaded with my sister to bring my son in. She said that he was asleep in bed and it was too late to bring him in. I got more and more upset on the phone and one nurse came, she took me off the phone and offered my some sleeping tablets, which I took.

I was in a dormitory-type ward and the woman in the bed next to me had a doll, which she called her baby. At approx. 2-3 in the morning she woke me up saying, 'Have you seen my baby? – I lost my baby – help me find my baby.'

Being woken up suddenly by a person who had lost her 'Baby' after I was separated and could not see my own baby was soul-destroying. And this was my introduction to Whitchurch Hospital as a patient.

Tracy Hartwell

Behind Grey Walls

As I grew up it was usual to hear someone say, 'I'm going mad, I am going to end up in Whitchurch.' My mother often said to my sisters and me 'You are going to drive me into Whitchurch.' Consequently the words 'Whitchurch Hospital' conjured up a place of horror and dread, where mad people lived.

In January 2001 my husband was diagnosed with Alzheimer's. I cared for him at home for six years. My husband started to go out and was unable to find his way home. This happened a few times. Each time I informed the police, they would find him and bring him back. The last time it happened, one of the police officers who had brought him home advised me to speak to his consultant in the memory clinic.

An emergency appointment was made for my husband to attend the clinic on the 15th February 2007. His consultant psychiatrist, in all her wisdom, decided to have him admitted into Whitchurch Hospital, in her words 'for his own safety.' He was sectioned for twenty-eight days under the Mental Health Act. The day he was sectioned destroyed both our lives. When someone is sent to a psychiatric hospital under section they are taken away in a police van with two police officers in attendance. I cannot think of that day without crying.

The day my husband was taken away from me he weighed seventeen and a half stone. He was big, strong, and was still quite *compos mentis*. I cannot imagine how he felt, being taken to Whitchurch Hospital, locked into a secure ward, and not being allowed to come home. I was advised not to see him for a week. I realise now that I shouldn't have listened to the so-called experts, I should have gone with him. I know I was in shock but I will always feel guilty for taking him to the memory clinic that day. I will always blame myself for his incarceration. That day was only the beginning of our nightmare.

The first time I went to visit my husband in Whitchurch Hospital, it confirmed all my worst fears. Whitchurch Hospital is an ugly Victorian building, with thick grey walls. It isn't difficult to imagine the horrors these walls have witnessed. The wards my husband stayed in were shabby and soulless. The patients' sleeping quarters were disgusting, no privacy or comfort. The food was appalling. Murderers, rapists, paedophiles, any prisoners, no matter what their crime, are treated better than people with mental health problems, especially Alzheimer's/dementia patients, because they have no voice.

After my husband had been in hospital for twenty-eight days, his consultant psychiatrist applied for him to be sectioned for a further six months. This was granted. My family and I were never consulted regarding my husband's sectioning.

From the day my husband was admitted into Whitchurch Hospital they started medicating him, in my opinion over-medicating. He was given a chemical cosh everyday which included three different anti-psychotic drugs. He was given these drugs at least three times a day. Within six months my husband had lost six stone in weight, one stone a month. He became doubly incontinent, shuffled when he walked, and was totally incoherent. This was a direct result of the medication he was forced to take. Prisoners have a right to decide what they put into their bodies, Alzheimer's/dementia patients do not. They certainly didn't in Whitchurch Hospital. I begged, pleaded, and demanded that the hospital psychiatrist reduce my husband's medication, to no avail. I discovered that these people have complete autonomy over your loved ones.

Most of the staff employed in the wards of Whitchurch Hospital that my husband stayed in are truly caring, kind, hardworking, and treat this low-paid job as a vocation. To them I have great respect, admiration, and deepest gratitude. But there are some who see the job and the patients as a monthly salary.

My husband is still in hospital. Obviously his illness has progressed but now he is in a wonderful hospital where all the staff are truly amazing. He is also, now, drug free.

Pauline Johnson

Love

You sat in your chair and I didn't recognize you anymore. You were picking up imagined fluff on the carpet. There was nothing to pick up but I agreed with you and helped you to pick up nothing.

I knew then I had to call my brother and we waited anxiously for the doctor to come. We both knew what this meant. Sadly this has happened before.

We took you to the hospital and I tried making small talk. You were scared and I was scared for you. I told you to see it as a chance to rest and to eat more regularly. You had neglected yourself. I buckled your seat belt and felt more like your mother than you being mine.

I spoke to the doctor and I spoke for you. The child in an old woman's body had returned again. I looked into your eyes and wished it could be different for us all. I wanted to protect you from yourself and make it all better again.

They agreed too and decided that you had to stay for a while. I felt immediate relief and sadness. You'd stopped taking your medication so it was only a matter of time.

Your whole life and ours has been like this. You have had little peace or happiness. So it follows neither did we.

I came every day to visit and you were always pleased to see me. I looked at the others and felt for them too. As time went by you started to get better and your mischievous smile came back. The medication was working. I had my mother back.

You made me laugh one day, you told me you asked the doctor if he felt OK, if he knew who the prime minister was, and if he was aware of what day it was? You were well again.

I am thankful for places like the hospital and the support it has given us through the years. I know you may one day have to return. Today your mind seems restless and sad. So I wait for the call.

Things happen and words get exchanged in moments of illness and sadness. One truth remains, Love is often tough but always heals. One day your mind will be peaceful. As will mine then.

Paula Windust

Memories

When I was quite young my Mum and Dad would often take me for a walk on a Sunday. We would go over the 'Five Fields' – then through the kissing gates. The fields are houses and roads now, and Manor Way was not completed, only just started.

As we were going through the fields we always met a few men who were inmates of Whitchurch Hospital. We would smile at them and they would nod back to us. Walking on we would get to the hospital. Then we would have a slightly different route back. On the way we would pass by a broken-down old building (like a big old house) which had a lovely fig tree in the garden; you could see the figs when it was the right season.

After a few years, towards the later part of the war, we started going over to Whitchurch Hospital to take the wounded boys their Sunday tea. Every Sunday we would go to the door to get to the wards. At the doorway was a very big and tall man – he was an 'inmate' of the hospital. We could go past him through the door, but the visitors would be arriving from all over the country to see their loved ones and he would say 'threepence to go in' – and they all seemed to give it to him. He did very well and nobody questioned him about it. He did not ask us as he knew we were bringing the 'eats.'

My husband was wounded but he was sent to a hospital in Newcastle and the boys and men in the hospital were from Newcastle, London, and all sorts of other places.

My grandfather used to work on the railway and he would tell me when a new lot of wounded boys came in, as he spent most of his time around the Whitchurch railway tapping the lines that meant more cakes to take over on the Sunday.

Years later, a good friend of mine had a nervous breakdown and she was taken to the hospital. She was in quite a state and was there for quite a while. I used to visit her every week and each week you could see she was getting better. She spoke very highly of the staff who looked after her.

The last time I visited the hospital was many years later when I went to visit a boyfriend I met in the City Hall, one evening at a dance. We went out together for a few months, then quite suddenly I realised he had problems. He was taken to Whitchurch Hospital and they started giving him electrical treatment. He was all right for a couple of weeks, then he went back into the hospital again. This went on for quite a while but eventually I was told to get out of this relationship as quickly as I could. He did eventually get worse and they sent him to Bridgend Hospital which was then a mental hospital. I never saw or heard about him after that.

Phyllis Hassell

Chaplaincy

I've been here fourteen years as hospital chaplain. A mixture of images: fear, anxiety, hope, healing, wholeness. Above all Whitchurch is a very safe environment where people can find security to express themselves.

A very hard-working and caring staff who rarely see people, especially the elderly, restored to health. Daunting and frustrating, yet so challenging and ironically rewarding.

The centenary service in 2009. Brother Brian, my Catholic colleague, and I arranged an inter-faith service at Tŷ Canol at which Dr Delyth Alldinck, Senior Consultant, gave a very moving address. As the centenary candle was lit on the altar by one of the patients it was extraordinary to witness that mental pain unites all religions of the world.

Since joining the Trust the hospital has been transformed physically, emotionally, and spiritually. Ten years ago our Chaplaincy Centre was blessed by the Bishop and is still in frequent use.

Whitchurch Hospital is like a large family. Sometimes dysfunctional and frustrating but for most of the time purposefully led and managed and aiming for excellence.

The sights, sounds, smells, tastes, and textures of hospital life …

Beautiful grounds, sometimes peaceful but also bad days of great disruption and fear; those usually associated with people who are sadly mentally ill; the refectory/canteen is very good; big improvement in furniture and structure.

I am here mostly in mornings and afternoons. Psychiatric hospitals are not great for visiting in the mornings, especially if people are not on the right drugs. The wards can appear a little drowsy in the afternoons.

It's definitely better in the spring and summer when patients with a variety of mental illness inevitably feel more upbeat. Autumn and winter see quite an upsurge in the numbers. Inclement weather rarely improves moods.

Canon Chancellor John H. L. Rowlands

Holidays by the Sea

As a sixteen-year-old girl in 1938, I came from Birmingham and had a meal in the medical quarters at Whitchurch – my brother was a doctor there. We were waited on by maids with white aprons and caps. I was so impressed. My brother, Bernant Phillips, had been a junior psychiatrist – he qualified at Cardiff – his first job was at Whitchurch. I adored my brother, he was so caring.

When I first saw the hospital, well, we walked in the grounds and there were some patients walking about in the garden. We went up the water tower – he said somebody had dropped his stethoscope down into the tower. We walked down those impressive corridors. We didn't go into the wards, just around and about. I had the idea that 'mad' people were dangerous and different. Seeing them *in situ* made me feel different.

I didn't see many chronic patients until I got to Whitchurch in 1948. They had recalcitrant wards – 'Don't send me to Fives' people would say. These were for the most difficult, violent patients. There were wards like that for men and women.

There were different dining rooms. The medics had their room, the nurses theirs, matron was served in her own room. As social workers, we were a bit of an odd body – we had an occupational therapist like us. We were served – no menu – but served by maids in uniform.

The patients were used to clean the corridors, to polish door handles. They took pride in their piece of corridor – long-stay patients, I'm talking about. This was the late forties, early fifties.

Keys – you had huge bunches of keys. You had to lock everything behind you – toilets etc. Enormous bunches. You felt like a jailor.

There were concerts and film. At Christmas time the staff performed pantomimes for the patients. Nurses also took patients off on holidays by the sea, of course they knew their patients – they lived with them. There was much that was caring and good.

Mair Piette

[This was after I had qualified as a psychiatric social worker in the Maudsley Hospital in London in 1948 when I joined the staff at Whitchurch having completed my degree in social science at Birmingham University.]

My life closed in on me today
i saw the futility of what THEY say
make hay while the sun shines
save for a rainy day
don't worry about tomorrow
for it never comes
what 'it' is
they never say

my life closed in on me yesterday
and tomorrow came with its worries
will anyone call at my door
will i be alone
like a pebble on the shore
will i be able to answer
that friend who calls to see
if everything's all right
if today i feel free
i'm tired of talking to doctors
who treat me like a kid
who presume in their arrogance
that somewhere in me's hid
a deep dark secret
of which i'm better rid

my life closed in on me finally
i saw the doctor clear
a neat demure existence
thirty, forty thousand a year
no worries paying bills
no! he sits secure
if he wants a sandwich
the occasional pint of beer
he doesn't have to worry
about starvation being near
he says i worry unduly
panic become manic depressed
but if he had my life
he'd know why i am stressed
on the outskirts of society
with a need in me
to be useful, to be recognised
to be freer, not be pressed
for pennies and ha'pennies
that make me dress in hand-me-downs
and jumble sale frumperies
that make me struggle daily
with skills so often slighted
till i see the world a fiction
as Shakespeare already cited
a stage with many players
who for all their faults
are slayers of no dragons
are heroes to the few
are philosophically naïve
are oft like me and you

but i sometimes do contort
my mind to think anew
it climbs into a structure
takes on tooth and nail
for the only way to learn
is to be there in chainmail
fighting with the dragons
fighting off the pale
of apathy, of i see me
who the hell are you
to sit there in your office
saying i should not be blue
without telling what colour
would perfectly suit you

yes

my life closed in on me
a decade or so ago
and i've been putting up with you
and your nowhere to go
you can't understand my insecurities
my questions want to know
my worries like the fact that
last time i wrote a poem
my life
crashed in around me
at sea without a home
is this the start of
another !
another ! !
another ! ! !
another breakdown

you see
you can't understand this position
you can't see it from your easy chair
where you are the huntsman
and my mind a fox in its lair
you sniff around the entrance
thinking you see it all
or you sit there smugly
not even trying, the gall!
we come to you for assistance
sometimes were even sent
you tell us to help ourselves
but take this 'cause your minds are bent
i went to see you yesterday
tried to crash your life
but walked out frustrated
you failed to see my strife
you failed to come to tea that time
you haven't seen where i live
but your middle-class existence
your smug security
is the cause that stops me being free
my life crushed in completely
a heap upon the floor
making an unsightly mess
emotions to the fore
i spewed out all my anger
cried
berated myself
and you sat
said
try this drug
that should make you see more sense

my life crushed in on me further
pain and panic and chemicals
but
you persist in your consumptive squalor
that keeps me in poverty
i used to dream of millions
but
now i dream of thirty pee
so that i might have some milk
in my weak cup of tea
you drink real coffee
cheese four pound a pound
live in rural dignity
without the city sound
that causes your life to crush me
pound by pound
for every coin that i have
every hundred pee
you have twenty, thirty, eighty times
that stops me being free

Roger Gilbert

Written in 1989

*This poem originally appeared in large scale format on the
wall of ward East 5A in Whitchurch Hospital.*

Whitchurch Hospital 1969-1971

I love mental hospitals, particularly the ones built in the years around the turn of the nineteenth to the twentieth century. It was obviously a time of prosperity and philanthropic certainties. The asylums were little worlds of their own. They had farms and kitchen gardens, their own orchestras and theatres where staff and patients could mix in a self-sufficient appearance of democracy. Outsiders often commented on how hard it was to tell the inmates and staff apart. Sometimes caring for the insane was an inherited job; generations of nurses. I suppose that, as my mother was a psychiatrist, I also followed this pattern. In some ways we all fitted too well into a very strange and abnormal environment.

My first impression was how closely it resembled most of those I had visited or worked in. A style you might call 'Palace of the Sun Emperor' as if the delusions of grandeur of the inmates were shared by the town planners.

Coming into Whitchurch Hospital from the front is impressive. Laid out as the view from the windows were large green areas for cricket and bowls and a sense of luxury and space. Once inside, the luxurious area of mahogany and dusty opulence was confined to the board room and other official areas across the front of the imposing porch, to be instantly counteracted by the cream and green institution paint of the corridors and wards and the faint smell of boiling greens.

Anyone who lives or works in a big institution makes small alliances. Tiny acts of mutual kindness make the life bearable.

I found Whitchurch to be in many ways rather insular and backward compared with the facilities of the places in which I had been working.

Our early hopes for keeping patients in the community were high but did not produce the brave new world we had expected. The process of 'freeing' the patients was very slow, hindered by poorly trained nursing staff, inadequate funding, entrenched public attitudes, and the nature of their illnesses. Although much has improved, particularly for those with learning disabilities, the country has never invested the necessary amounts of cash and energy to give dignity of life to people with chronic mental health problems.

One thing that really annoyed me in those days was that the board of governors met every month in Whitchurch Hospital. They read a report from the matron and the medical superintendent and discussed policy. Now I had, and have, no quarrel with that. I am an unusual person in that I will freely admit to enjoying meetings, if well conducted. Even the less good ones afford a welcome change from being on one's feet and rushing around trying to catch an ever-receding hare, probably a mad March one in our line of work. It's a good corrective for individual tyranny and makes for consensus management.

No, what I objected to was that they always had a very good lunch. Briefly the smell of boiled greens would be replaced by more delicious odours at the front of the hospital, wafting from the mahogany mausoleum.

'Why can't they have what the patients on the chronic wards are getting?' I would cry to shocked, uncomprehending looks. Alas, no one was in the least interested in my French Revolutionary moments; a sort of reverse 'Let them eat cake.'

There were always rumours of untoward things that

went on. There was supposed to be a poker school that met secretly in the linen room of one of the wards. Everyone knew about the occasional alcoholic nurse, sipping regularly from a concealed bottle.

The night superintendent at that time was firm but fair, and I enjoyed many a cup of tea and gossip with her. One night she had apparently annoyed someone. I was in the office when she came in, in tears. Her car had been opened and the whole contents of the hospital dustbins poured inside. The mess was horrible; clearly done by a staff member, not a patient.

Elinor Kapp

Concerns

As a student nurse in the day hospital we were told to be aware of people who were 'low in mood', because they might attempt to self-harm.

I went to the toilet on my way to lunch. The doors there had their bottoms cut away for observational purposes and I could see a set of shoes almost protruding from the space. They weren't moving. I washed my hands and left the toilet, still feeling concerned so, I went back in. The shoes still hadn't moved. So I asked, 'Who's there, please?' No answer. I asked again – no answer so I knocked on the door, repeating 'Who's there?'

'It's Dr Llewellyn!,' came the answer. 'Go away!'. I beat a hasty retreat to the hospital canteen!

Mike Jones

History Snapshots – 3

Throughout 1898 and the early months of 1899 Cardiff Borough Council was intent on finding land on which to build a mental hospital – Cardiff City Asylum as it was originally known. It was not an easy task as the Commissioners in Lunacy (who would give approval to any scheme) had already laid down certain exacting specifications.

The hospital would have to be outside the boundaries of Cardiff itself, on land that was open and offering a 'cheerful' prospect for patients. And yet it had to be close enough to offer access to the people from the community it was meant to serve.

Pentyrch, Radyr, Penarth, and Rhoose were among several possible locations but when, in October 1899, part of the Velindre estate at Whitchurch was offered to the council – at a price of just over £200 an acre – it was quickly decided that this 120 acre site was exactly what was required. The site included the old Velindre mansion house and two farms, Tŷ Clyd and Llwyn Mallt.

The firm of Oatley and Skinner, architects from Bristol, won the competition to design the new hospital and in 1902 the foundations were laid by Cardiff contractor D. W. Davies. The building work was taken forward by the firm of William King and Sons from London.

The hospital building was intended to care for 750 patients, 336 of them male, 414 female. Over the ten years that it took to create, a horse-shoe style, two-storey building was erected with a classical entrance porch on the north face. Banded brickwork and copper cupolas on

117

the top of the ventilation ducts broke up what could otherwise be called a rather severe facade.

The hospital was dominated by the 150-foot water tower, noticeable from many miles around. Wards were laid out in ten blocks with dayrooms and dormitories and a number of single rooms. The provision of verandahs gave staff the ability to extend the wards if it was felt to be appropriate.

There were workshops for trades such as carpentry and tailoring, sewing rooms, and laundry facilities – all of which were intended to make the hospital as self sufficient as possible. Accommodation was also provided for nursing staff while the medical superintendent was given a detached house set within the hospital grounds.

A hospital chapel was built close to the main entrance, providing seating for at least 800 people while exercise gardens and a large hall were also provided to help with the recreational needs of patients and staff.

Dr Edwin Goodall was appointed medical superintendent in 1906, two years before the hospital was completed. He used the time to organise the staff and equip the establishment appropriately – at a cost that caused some concern to the council and to the rate payers of Cardiff.

Inevitably, alterations had to be made to many of the original plans, the greatest change coming when opposition to the extensive farm buildings rose to a fury in the local press. The proposed piggery, originally planned to cost £4000, was severely reduced, much to the disgust of Dr Goodall who had always believed in the therapeutic value of farm work. In the end the hospital still cost £349,000 to build, an enormous sum in the early years of the twentieth century.

Councillor Morgan Thomas formally opened the hospital on 15th April 1908, invited guests being given a tour of the new facilities. The first fifty patients arrived on

1st May that year.

Phil Carradice
Author, historian and lead writer on The Whitchurch
Project

First Death

The first death I saw was at Whitchurch. There was an extremely ill man lying in a ward bed. I saw him moving his head slowly, appearing to follow something with his eyes on the ceiling. His gaze had just reached the end of the ceiling, when he suddenly and sadly smiled and died. Later, screens were pulled the around the bed – reverence was of utmost importance. I next heard the sound of singing from behind the screens. One of the nurses was singing a hymn as he began to perform last offices on the gentleman who had died. We'd been taught reverent silence, but here he was, singing. At the time I thought it was wrong but later, on reflection, I realised it was quite a respectful and, arguably, an appropriate act. It was the first time I had encountered the, at times, contradiction between theory and the reality of practice.

Mike Jones

Perspective

Invisible, gliding the passages of this building. Scenes are framed by windows. Smooth, deep green comes into view, rich and glossy. I draw in closer to the high window pane. Looking out, there are three stone steps and a dark wooden door, laden with panelling and metal brackets.

Above the door is a wrought-iron lamp, paint peeling from the metal. The steps are shaped into curves where the stone has worn. They lead to the thick green carpet below. The door looks like it has not been opened for a long time and the grass at the bottom of the steps is undisturbed.

Stretching, standing on my toes, I see a greenhouse and an open grow-bag with some nearly ripe tomatoes. I think there must be another way to get out there, separate to the door with the iron lamp, but I can't see another door from this angle. There are patio chairs and tables dotted around. They're mottled and muddy but I think they're still used.

There are no flowers but the scene is fresh in its greenness, fertile with the ripe fruit. The grass twinkles in the sunlight, ignited by a sprinkle of light rain a few hours ago. It offers me hope and nourishment. I feel hopeful.

Slipping back into the shadows of the corridor, I turn onto the curve. It brings me back towards the heart of the building like a rib ... cold, hard, and structured, offering protection to the inner core. One man passes with a slight tilt of the head but he doesn't look me in the eye.

I float past scenes of outside, inner courtyards framed by the windows. As I turn towards each window, a thin transparent veil separates me from those images of the outside world – the image of me looking back at myself in the reflection, expression changing in response to the images I encounter, in response to the image of my reflection itself.

The curve ends and I'm back on a straight stretch. I'm drawn to the jungle ahead. From some distance, I see a mass of entangled limbs of brambles and wild grasses, twisting and grabbing at every opportunity at the disused parts of the building, now neglected and sometimes abused. The weeds have worked themselves into a messy knot, tying themselves irrevocably to one another.

There is a door. I press my nose and hands flat against it and my reflection disappears. The jungle beast consumes old tins of paint, a small figure of superman, some bed sheets, and a rusty barbeque. What else is out there? There is more but I can't make sense of the shapes and colours I pick out. When did it get like this? How did it happen?

With one step back, my reflection gives me insight into feelings of confusion, fear, and doubt, far removed from the hope I felt just two passages away. I feel physical pain as I retreat backwards. I look down and the brambles have reached through the crack in the door, across the floor, scratching at my ankles.

As I turn my back to the scene, a drop of blood trails down onto the floor, another blotch on its tainted pattern. I must move on. I have much work to do and can't pause for long. My time here is limited.

Hollie Edwards-Davies

Post-Mortem and Mortuary

During the early 1960s I discovered that post-mortem examinations on elderly patients who had died after many years – sometimes decades – as long-stay residents, were performed by the senior male nurse manager, (Mr H.), who was then over sixty-five years old.

He had trained as a post-mortem technician in keeping with the encouragement given at the time to staff to obtain additional qualifications.

He became so skilled in this function that medical staff allowed him to dissect the bodies unsupervised and prepare samples for their later attention. They would examine his notes and opinions, all entered in copperplate handwriting in a large heavy volume, and use his conclusions when they made their official report.

I watched him on two occasions. The first was of a man I had personally cared for in his final days. It was strange to see his organs removed and his body reduced to a shell. It was also a superb 3D anatomy lesson.

The interior of the P.M./Mortuary building had not changed since it was constructed. The fittings – cupboards, P.M. slabs, wash basins, etc., were all the originals. The dissecting equipment was heavy Victorian brass and stainless steel, beautifully kept.

The mortuary section was austere with just a few slate slabs and wooden head-rests in separate rooms for male and female bodies. A tiny chapel-like room was fitted out to allow relatives to view a body in private. There was a velvet cushion for the head-rest and a rich cloth pall to cover the body.

Before I finished at Whitchurch I made a point of going to places and rooms I'd worked in, some of which I hadn't visited for years. In the mortuary, I saw that the book Mr G. made his entries in was still there, in the preparation room – even though the room had not been used for decades. I opened the book and found the entry for that first post-mortem that I had watched so many years ago. I opened the cupboard and drawers but the dissecting tools had long disappeared.

I looked in the main mortuary and saw that some wit had scrawled, in chalk, on a name-board above one of the slabs: 'Reserved for Keith Sullivan'.

Keith Sullivan

Memories

We had so many laughs whilst in the nursing office. We had a number of minibuses which staff drove to take patients on trips, or to appointments. We had a booking system for these buses which was run through nursing office. A nurse who shall
remain nameless took one of the buses out one day and on returning to the front hall to hand back the keys to us saw a guy standing there. He said, 'Are you waiting for the bus?' thinking he was from OT and had booked the bus after him. The guy said yes and he handed the keys to him. The guy in question happened to be a patient who had been admitted after trying to drive a car up the steps of the museum in town. First wind we got of it was when his wife in Ely rang up to ask why was her husband home and what was a Whitchurch Hospital minibus doing outside her house! The story didn't end there because next day we had a call from someone in the Welsh office complaining that they had been cut up on Ely roundabout by a Whitchurch Hospital minibus the day before!

Another time we had a call in Central Nursing Office to say that a man had gone berserk in a car in the hospital grounds and was driving it erratically around the place, knocking over benches and such like. On occasions such as this men were summoned from the Forensic Unit to attend. We looked out of our office window on the front of the hospital overlooking the bowling green to see a large Volvo car approaching from the church end – it bounced down on to the bowling green, careered across it, up the other side, over the rockery, just missing a bench, and came to a halt outside our office. Turned out he was one of the hospital bowlers, a retired butcher, and he had just taken delivery of this automatic car and had completely lost control of it. He stepped out of the car looking rather shaken, along with his dog who looked quite excited. We then noticed the man only had one arm – seems he lost it in a meat slicer accident when he had his butcher's shop, so all in all, not a very lucky individual.

Film makers were always interested in using the hospital buildings as backdrops to productions and one day we were visited by a broadcasting team with Anthony Hopkins. Great excitement. They were using the outside of the building as a Victorian boys' school for the production they were doing. Excited at the thought of Sir Anthony being on the premises, I decided along with my colleague, to take a trip over to the farm buildings where they were based to see if we could get his autograph. I knew the back way around the farm so off we went. Well, sad to say, we didn't even get a glimpse of him but determined not to look stupid, we got back to the office and I got a piece of paper on which I wrote 'To Ann, Best wishes, Anthony Hopkins' and left it on the desk for all to see. People were mightily impressed – they had no idea what his signature looked like. Anyway, we had to come clean in the end but it was a good laugh while it lasted.

The board room used to be used for mental health review tribunals and it was next door to our office. On tribunal days the patients being reviewed along with their carers and solicitor would congregate outside the office waiting to be called in. We were sitting working one day when we could hear one of our lovely elderly patients saying over and over again 'I love you, I love you, I love you'. We recognised immediately who it was and went out to see who she was talking to. What a laugh. There was a solicitor, suited and booted, briefcase in hand sitting on the bench waiting to be called, and here was our lovely patient sitting on his lap kissing him and whispering sweet nothings in his ear. He was petrified.

Ann Sullivan

A Day in the Life

There was always an early wake-up call at around 8 a.m., which might sound annoying, however, the prospect of a ready-cooked breakfast was quite an incentive to get up, and it was always nice to see which other staff and patients were already awake. Perhaps too, in my state of being 'high', getting up was easier because of this.

Getting dressed was a bit different here as well. It also involved checking that things like your watch hadn't been stolen in the night.

Maybe you'd have a game of pool. The pool tables on the wards were always in really poor condition but you would adapt your game to match the table. By the end of a couple of months' stay, you'd be pretty much an expert. The nurses, therefore, who'd of course been there for years, were practically world class.

There would usually be at least one other person already in the smoking room. It is still legal to smoke indoors in psychiatric hospitals, and the smoking room is always a hub of activity. Smoking has a great deal of benefits for patients in a place like this. It is a good way of relieving tension, as well as passing the time. The smoking room itself becomes a very good place for social interaction. All kinds of conversations will take place, from just general chat to discussions about religion. There was a Bible in the smoking room the last time I was there, and many patients can get quite deeply into religious thought. The smoking room could become thick with smoke, and the smell could be quite overpowering – even when going into it when the ashtrays had been emptied in

128

the mornings – but for me, these places were essential for many patients.

If it was the day of my doctor's ward round, I would spend twenty minutes or so trying to persuade him to take me off section and let me go. I never quite worked out what he wanted me to say or do to prove my eligibility for release but what generally happened was that the more leave I had, the more I showed I could cope while on leave, the more likely it would be that I would be taken off section.

I have to say that there were some nurses who I would genuinely say saved my life at times. There were also some not-so-pleasant nurses, but a lot of them proved that it takes a certain kind of person to work for the NHS – there really are some genuinely caring people in the service, who restore any faith you may have lost in humanity. Even if it was simply someone to talk to, some of the nurses could be fantastic, and made me laugh out loud so often. I wouldn't say the same for the doctors, though, who frankly never seemed to care too much – they prescribed the drugs, and that was about it, as far as I could tell.

Three or four times a day, the nurses would administer these drugs, usually after meal times. The food at Whitchurch was generally pretty good, with quite a good variety. I always looked forward to fish and chips on Friday. I have to say though, Whitchurch Hospital was actually the reason why I stopped being a vegetarian during an admission around twenty years ago. My mum had brought me in a cheese and onion pasty from Greggs, but I asked her if instead she could get me a Big Mac. Due to this indiscretion, it was decided that I was not a vegetarian, and they refused to serve me vegetarian food from then on. I don't mind in some ways, as I do like the taste of meat, and I really would struggle to go back to being vegetarian now.

Due to being on medication though, you would quite often still be hungry, especially in the evenings, and you, or someone on your behalf would quite often have to go out to the Spar just outside of the hospital entrance to get extra supplies. If I missed lunch, I would quite often get a sandwich as they made fresh sandwiches there; cheese and sweet chilli sauce became a favourite of mine.

Filling the time would always be an issue in Whitchurch. I watched quite a bit of TV; I listened to my Walkman quite a bit, sometimes while taking a walk around the hospital – I would try to get some exercise – but there were still large sections of the day that needed filling. Sometimes I would go into Whitchurch village itself, just to get out and look around. I might get a haircut, or buy little things to brighten the day. Walks into the village were another way of getting more accustomed to life outside again.

There were quite a lot of organised activities. Some people did not bother with these at all, but I would be quite involved. I enjoyed the art sessions, and would usually have a project that I worked on. The sports activities were quite good – I played football and volleyball. There were a few quite reasonable players who got really into it, but anyone of any ability was encouraged to get involved. One time when I was in, I had seen that there was a 5k run for charity taking place in Barry a few months after I'd been admitted, and I set myself the goal of being fit enough for this in time for when I hoped I'd be released. I went to the gym a couple of days a week, and was extremely grateful to one of the physios who put in some extra time to help get me trained, and even took me out for short runs to build me up for the event. I went from being barely able to run more than a few hundred metres to being prepared for the event, which I did take part in, finishing around halfway up the field. The physio who had helped with my training came eighth, I think, out of around 400!

The last time I was in, I actually had four different girlfriends – not all at the same time! – so I would hang out with them at times, although how appropriate these relationships were in a hospital context, I'm not really sure!

In the evenings, I would get visits from friends and family. They would usually come shortly after the evening meal, but after I'd been waiting for them for perhaps the whole day, I could sometimes become quite frustrated, especially when I was still not very well, and these visits did not always go that well. It could sometimes be quite difficult understanding what was still going on in the real world that visitors would talk about. Talk of sport was so often a good way of bringing you down to earth – I know it was a favourite topic of conversation for a lot of the male nurses.

Just occasionally while in hospital, I would go to the pub, even though this was not really allowed. I would not drink much however. After having been a month or two without any alcohol, drinking could be quite problematic, especially while medicated, and quite often, just a half of beer could make me feel quite peculiar, so I didn't do it too often.

Finally, it would be time to go to bed. I would sometimes listen to the radio before settling down. There were sometimes patients who would make a fair bit of noise and disturb your sleep. Sometimes, I would just not be able to sleep, but sometimes, I would be allowed to have a 'sleeper', i.e. something like valium. They didn't like you taking these too often, as they didn't want you to get addicted. But finally I might settle down – just another day in the life of a Whitchurch patient.

Nick Fisk

Alarm

We set off the 'fire alarm' and got trapped in the corridors. Fearing what we had done we couldn't move – we both just froze! Then, a while later, I just saw these huge wellingtons and slowly I looked up. As I did, I saw another pair of huge wellingtons. As I gradually looked up at both men I started to tremble. Then one of the staff from our ward arrived and said 'There you are! We've been looking everywhere for you.' The two firemen tapped us on the shoulder and said 'You won't do that again, will you?' We both agreed and were taken back to our ward. Whenever I hear the alarm go I always remember that guilty moment in my past.

Elizabeth Kemble

Do you see what I see?

Do you see what I see?
Someone who's ill
Or another who kills?
Do you look inside a 'bloke'
Or see him sniffing coke?

Do you see what I see?
A psychiatric ward,
And all who stay there look bored, pained, and grieved.
Do you see what I see?
An old man, just wheeled out dead.

He had suffered a long time with depression,
Until he had had enough.
Why not die you say?
He was old anyway.

Do you feel what I feel?
Or are your ears still closed.

Do you hear what I hear?
Screams in the night
Just another 'drugged up psycho.'

Do you see what I see?
Can you set these people free?

Angelo David Gauci

There Were Beech Trees

There were beech trees, sycamores, and oaks, providing us not only with outstanding russets and fiery orange hues, but also chestnuts, mahogany, shiny treasures in spiky green jackets, acorns in little cups, and swirly plane pods. There were pine trees and their cones.

I can remember the beautiful flower beds: dahlias, roses, all flowers in their seasons. I especially remember the purple, white, and orange crocuses and the snowdrops around the church. Also the holly and rowan trees with their red berries.

If you felt better you could appreciate all these things but in a deep depression they meant nothing, no matter how much people would tell you how 'lucky' you were to be surrounded by them!

Ann Cummings Teear

History Snapshots – 4

By the early summer of 1908 the City of Cardiff Mental Hospital (Whitchurch Hospital as it became) had already admitted 340 male patients, 271 female, a staggering admission rate considering the place had been open only for a few short months. And from the start Dr Goodall was clear that Whitchurch was not to be just an asylum but a hospital 'where treatment and care would alleviate and cure.'

Goodall was a man of great vision but he could have not have achieved anything without a dedicated and professional workforce. He was assisted by thirty-eight nurses, forty-five male attendants, and a number of assistants and administrative staff.

It was, in those early days, an efficient and effective establishment that earned great praise from the Commissioners in Lunacy. In particular the hospital was praised for its use of open-air treatment and the care and compassion shown by staff – care and compassion that went well beyond the usual mental-health provision of the time.

The hospital had operated for only a few short years when the world went to war in the summer of 1914. The conflict had a dramatic effect on everyone in the country but in 1915 the work of the hospital was totally disrupted when, with casualty figures gradually mounting and the need for hospital beds becoming urgent, it was handed over to the military.

Patients were immediately sent off to other institutions in various parts of the country. The effect of such treatment on men and women with severe mental health problems and illnesses can only be imagined but the action has to be viewed in the context of the time. Britain needed hospital beds and Whitchurch had many to offer. For the rest of the war Whitchurch operated as a general medical hospital, hundreds of men arriving for recuperation and treatment – and for surgery.

Dr Edwin Goodall remained in charge of the hospital and when, once the war ended in 1918 and the hospital returned to Cardiff Borough administration, he was at the helm to pick up the pieces and start again.

Throughout the 1920s the reputation of Whitchurch continued to grow. A high proportion of the nurses gained qualifications in both general and mental-health nursing, Dr Goodall introducing an in-service training programme that was the envy of many other hospitals. The life of a nurse at Whitchurch during these years was far from easy, however. Nurses regularly worked almost sixty hours a week. They had to live at the hospital and their daily existence was governed by a range of harsh rules and regulations that now seem almost spartan in their inflexibility.

When Dr Goodall finally retired in 1929 he could pride himself in having created an establishment that was a leader in its field. Research was regularly being carried out at the hospital into the causes and treatment of mental illness and in an age when the stigma of such illness remained enormous, Whitchurch was very much a show place.

Phil Carradice
Author, historian and lead writer on The Whitchurch Project

I remember the screams, early in the morning during meds.
I remember the windows – large and long.
I remember the blood-stained carpet.
I remember tea and toast at supper – the only food I ever ate.
I remember Phil dunking toast in his coffee.
I remember the sun flooding through all those windows.
I remember weak, tasteless coffee.
I remember the alcoholmeter.
I remember having a bath to stay warm.
I remember the lady in the next bed snoring loudly.
I remember the gentleman who forgot to get dressed.
I remember Allan so drugged up he needed ZNA to help him walk.
I remember feeling well enough to be able to pick a coin up for an older lady.
I remember the clatter of cutlery being laid out.
I remember hearing *Call My Bluff* from the lounge T.V. for the first time.
I remember the grand, pine, Welsh dresser.
I remember the dew and crisp air on my day of admittance.
I remember cats sneaking into E1.
I remember the bench outside E1 where I used to hide.
I remember the dingy male dorm at night.
I remember the feeling of acceptance.
I remember the patient-peer support and non-judgement.
I remember nurses flipping the window slats on the nightly obs.
I remember the pharmacy latch stinking of potions.
I remember the clatter of keys and doors slamming.
I remember feeling safe.

I remember my emotions starting to creep back in.
I remember the nurses' office, never daring to knock the door and disturb their party.
I remember the flowery sofas, dirty yet so inviting.
I remember E1 and the dark, unloved lounge.
I remember the chairs in the E1 lounge – rough and itchy.
I remember the excitement of all the female staff with the firemen striding along the corridor downstairs, hoping they'd come into our ward.
I remember the fire alarm many times a day.
I remember collecting conkers from those grand sycamore trees.

Maddy Read

Overture and Beginners – October 13th 1968

'Ram! Ram!' The shout echoed around the corridors of the male nurses' home.

Ram? Ram? The only rams I knew of were either male sheep or, and here my concern peaked sharply, those males of a high sexual proclivity. Was the shout a warning or, heaven forbid, a request? What had I let myself in for?

Only six hours earlier, I was nestled in the midst of cosy familiarity, inside the small terraced house of my Rhondda childhood. Family and neighbours had gathered to wish me well as I prepared to confront my future as a student psychiatric nurse in the bright lights and moral hazards of Cardiff. Adventure indeed for a young Valleys lad, stuffed full of the non-conformist values of a mining community, who was known to become homesick – even at the bottom of the street!

Two hours later, perched on the top deck of a Rhondda Transport bus, I spied the landmark water tower of Whitchurch Hospital, silhouetted against the setting October sun. Anticipation and apprehension increased, as one life chapter was about to end and another begin.

I walked through the imposing, twin stone pillars of the hospital entrance and made my way along the rustling, leaf-covered driveway, dragging a battered, ancestral suitcase packed with comfort blankets of every kind. Arriving at the hospital foyer, I recall the formality of it all.

The whole internal fabric was clad in dark wood panelling, with a multi-coloured mosaic-tiled floor and an overwhelming nostalgic smell of lavender polish. I introduced myself to the switchboard operator and was asked to wait until the on-duty deputy matron arrived to take me to my room. Matron?! The very word fanned my anxiety. No doubt a formidable, robust, Carry On-esque lady, with a military bark and sharp, brusque manner. A few minutes later and the first stereotype was demolished (many more would scatter like skittles in the days and months to come). A male deputy matron! A male! A friendly man, with a ruddy complexion, topped with a froth of neatly combed fair hair. He was smartly dressed in a black suit and, I recall, a bright red tie. 'Mr Jones?' he asked, nasally. I think I smiled, shyly. 'I'm Mr McHugh, deputy matron.' He smiled and shook my hand. It was the first time that anyone had called me 'mister'. It felt strange and inappropriate. Surely I was too young to be called 'mister'?

'I'll take you to your room.' He had a familiar 'valley' accent, and this common ground encouraged me to feel a little more comfortable.

We walked along what seemed like miles of twisting corridors, the walls half-clad in highly polished, brown and green ceramic tiles. The male nurses' home was equally as formal. Two corridors with polished wooden floors, partially covered in patterned carpet runners, with rows of dark, thickly-varnished oak room doors running along one side of their length.

My room was a great disappointment. Tucked in a cul-de-sac off one corridor, it was even darker and smaller than my bedroom at home. Even the light bulb struggled to brighten it. I contemplated, momentarily, whether moving into my suitcase might have been a roomier alternative. The living space was furnished with a dark brown, single wardrobe in one corner and a white china sink in the other. There was a single bed wedged behind the door, while the only enlightenment was a small complimentary packet of digestive biscuits and several coffee sachets, placed on an antique dressing table that filled the length of the remaining wall. The deputy-matron smiled. In the dimness, I couldn't quite make out if it was from politeness or pity.

A few steps took Mr McHugh across the length of room to the window.

'This is the fire escape.' He lifted the droop of yellowing net curtain, before wrestling with the bottom window sash until it eventually opened with a submissive creak. The room became infested with the odour of boiled cabbage, accompanied by a discordant chorus of loud clanging and an occasional human voice.

'The yard of the hospital kitchen is down there.' Mr McHugh, still smiling, moved away from the window, indicating the outside with a flick of his head.

I moved over to the sill and peered out, expecting to see a sturdy stairway that, in the event of a conflagration, would guide me safely to the flagstones some twenty feet below. Instead, there were only the flagstones some twenty feet below!

'Where's the fire escape?' I asked, puzzled, yet maintaining a tone of polite enquiry.

'You walk along the plank.' I thought it was a hospital, not a pirate ship.

A length of wood about twelve inches wide bridged the chasm. One end rested on my windowsill, and the other on the sill of a window some yards away. The plank didn't look strong enough to hold itself up, let alone a cherubic, seventeen stone nineteen-year-old with acrophobia. What a choice. I made a quick mental note to practise bed-sheet knotting.

'You'll be on ward East 3A for the time being. Report to Mr Haver, the charge nurse, at nine o'clock in the morning. He'll look after you'. Mr McHugh moved towards the room door. He handed me two large, weighty door keys attached to a metal ring. With a smile of feigned satisfaction, I thanked him, and he left with final instructions on where to obtain an obligatory white coat.

'Ram! Ram!' The voice continued to grow in volume, and was now close to my room door. With my curiosity tweaked, I opened it and took a peep into the corridor. The voice was standing a few feet away; a short man, about my age. What disturbed me was his mini-skirt, fishnet, stockings and full make-up. He seemed agitated.

'Have you seen Ram?' Equally puzzling was, again, the lack of the definite or indefinite article. 'No. I'm sorry, I haven't.' He recognized I was a new arrival.

'I'm Roy. How long have you been here?'

'I'm Mike. About four hours.' We smiled and shook hands. I noted the lack of nail varnish.

'I'm looking for Ramsey. I've got a dress for him.' He held up what I assumed was a nurse's uniform. I pondered if I should leave for home immediately or simply barricade myself in my room and shout for help.

'Who?' I enquired.

'Ramsey. Ram. He should be here somewhere. I don't know his room number. There's a fancy-dress party in The Hollybush. Do you want to come?' Context brought relief. I declined the invitation, being already a little homesick and reeling from a degree of culture shock. Even the merest hint of transvestism, albeit part-time and flippant, would have curled the lips of the chapel fraternity and redoubled their prayers to protect me from Old Nick and his kinfolk, still at large in 'sin city'.

Having broken the ice, my confidence increased, and I decided to break out from the security of my room. The dimly lit corridors reeked of age and disinfectant. The very walls seemed coloured with the ghosts of hundreds of others who had taken the same path since 1908, the year the hospital officially opened.

I wandered apprehensively along one of the corridors. It terminated in a heavy, thickly varnished door stencilled

143

with the words 'Common Room', picked-out in large, gold-coloured letters. The muffled sound of a radio or television came from within. What were the rules of engagement? Should I knock politely or simply walk in unannounced? I tapped on the door. No reply. I knocked a second time, more boldly. Straining to listen, I failed to hear a response, which prompted a third, much louder knock.

'Come in!' shouted a voice. I opened the door and peered in.

He sat in a winged armchair, sipping from a wineglass. A gaunt man, dressed in a red paisley dressing gown and a blue and white polka-dot cravat. It seemed Cowardesque, a scene from *Private Lives*. Was he another participant in the fancy dress party?

'Come in. Sit down. My name's Gerald.' It wasn't his obvious, effeminate tone that made me feel somewhat uneasy, nor the lady-like way he held a cigarette. It was the accompanying smile and facial expression, which unnerved me. To my then prejudicial and naïve eye, it could only be described as 'leering'. I revised my initial impression. Not *Private Lives* but *Round the Horne*. Here was Julian! I smiled, made an excuse to leave, and returned briskly to my room, not wishing to be there if and when Sandy minced in.

And so to bed. On my first night away from home, I felt alone; cast adrift in an unfamiliar ocean, bereft of a compass. This was a different kind of solitude, an odd, finely balanced blend of excitement, acute apprehension, and not a little disillusionment. I slipped between the unfamiliar covers, knowing sleep would be a stranger as I awaited the beginning of my future on the morrow.

I still remember lying in the quiet dark. Outside, in the distance, a dog barked. Alone, forlorn, uncertain, afraid; the perceptions of someone about to enter the unknown, who has a powerful yearning for familiarity and certainty;

a yearning for home. What were they doing at home? Watching television? My sister preening herself in front of her bedroom mirror, listening to Radio Luxembourg? My father dozing by the coal fire? Were they thinking about me? Worried about their son alone in the 'big city'? Or was I already becoming a distant memory; a ship that passed in the night? At the same time, a contradiction – the undoubted excitement and anticipation for the experiences to come.

The night continued. Somewhere a door slammed, a water pipe rattled, other alien sounds mingled with occasional muffled voices drifting along the corridors.

This initial experience taught me two immediate and valuable lessons. The first that everyone has a need to feel welcomed and cared about, listened to and, where necessary, to have a measure of guidance about what is expected. The second is never to make instant assumptions. Each experience needs to be considered and placed in its proper context.

A novel and somewhat surreal introduction to a career, my first real meander in the foothills of adulthood. A winding ascent of what would prove to be an endless mountain range, offering countless opportunities to become part of the lives, deaths, despairs, hopes, miseries and joys, achievements and disappointments of so many individuals.

Mike Jones

The Magician

I the magician must find the out-door before the wicked
bar and ban me
Time is important to escape the grasp of enemies within
Impossibility is not an option for sweet release is
necessary

My enemies are cunning, and wrap the spells in codes of
mumbled word lists
Schemes are drawn and drunk, and tasty food has
messages for my hungry brain and mind
Failure is not happening if I count backwards and wave the
shining wand of winning

Diving into fresh air is imperative and is the way to win
this
Circumnavigate the trap by ambulance, and here is exiting
I wrap up and roll out, undetected by smell, as the enemy
has travelled downwind

Police and friends bring maps and charts, and sensitivity
can be used in stronger way than theirs
Paint the white with dark and hide the stranger thoughts
with clever use of tasty trick and treat
Then leap in shining glory and the magic is complete and
whole and they have empty hands

Jane King

146

Whitchurch

A farmyard,
Blankness,
Everything nailed down,
No hangers for clothes,
Not enough bed-linen to keep you warm,
Threatening staff screaming at you because they are
understaffed,
Standing away from patients only talking to each other too
busy to talk or care for you,
No care in the environment,
Windows only opened to two inches,
Cold at night.
Patients throwing drinks in your face and being allowed to
do it by staff.
No trust given to you from staff.
Being screamed in my face by a male nurse having a go at
me when I chanted as part of my Buddhist practise, an
important aid to recovery,
Being branded a liar,
You get used to being locked in the ward and treated like
this. Then eventually you become passive in order to
leave, go home, or move on.

Anonymous

A Different Experience, Adfer Ward

The Adfer ward is run by CAU (Community Addiction Unit) for purposes of 'detox' for those wishing to abstain from substance misuse – in my case, alcoholism. It has much to recommend. It has extremely small bedrooms, a comfortable, communal seating area with TV and pool table, a kitchen for personal use at any time, bathrooms, a smoking room, and a staff office.

The atmosphere on Adfer was different to any other ward. There was a lot more freedom, in many ways, and group trips to Whitchurch 'Village' and quizzes were held too. However, the general hospital was still as depressing as ever, despite recent closures of some wards there, with the drab green corridors, dirty and smelling, full of chronically mentally-ill patients in the archaic institution. I did not feel I even had a mental illness, I was just adapting to my current health situation. The hospital shop staff, however, were as rude as ever!

In general, it all felt rather reminiscent of my first experience of Whitchurch Hospital in the main building. I visited it one day, feeling lost or confused, and was interviewed by a very homophobic psychiatrist who questioned me about my sexuality and went on to suggest a period of observation. However, at the sight of lobotomised-looking patients wandering around with mobility problems, I took off, petrified, and went home in such an upset state. I could not rest for two weeks! At that time, homosexuality was still considered to be a 'mental illness'.

On Adfer ward, staff attitudes were, on the whole, more open about LGBT lifestyles. Also, I found them very helpful – more so than I'd encountered on previous stays in the hospital. The ward psychiatrist, whom I only met the once, decreased my daily anti-psychotic dosage of Chlozapine. Obviously he was more on the ball than the psychiatrist at my local CMHT. Also, we had daily injections; drugs to combat alcohol and vitamins.

I just began drinking heavily when I moved into Supported Housing, usually to 'escape' the unpleasant house by visiting pubs – not the safest of places on one's own – or consumed cans in the local park. Often I was mistaken for a tramp.

Whilst a patient at Adfer, I did begin to feel better, more self-aware, and not in such a 'vegetative' state as at home. My stay was almost like a holiday. A friend visited and was very glad about my improved state, so obviously the ward and lack of alcohol were helping me in numerous ways.

My second stay at Adfer was more successful and constructive, having relapsed following my first admittance. I was more committed to the matter in hand and not so aware of the fact it was based in a disgusting psychiatric hospital. My first time I felt quite trapped, paranoid, threatened, and generally uneasy and also too anxious to attend TDP at Rebecca Suite. The ward had had a few small changes. I believe there is an abundance of self-fulfilling prophecy attitudes at places like Whitchurch Hospital, whereby, in adapting to the institution, a poor mental state can be induced, even if one isn't particularly mentally ill in the first place, as a result of integration and staff attitudes there.

Adfer ward is not so judgemental, nor did it practise any discrimination. Therefore I consider this a positive part of Whitchurch Hospital – perhaps the only one? It puts the rest to shame.

Diana Hodson

Taking Things for Granted

'Who said you could work here?'

'Linda, I suppose. The ward manager.'

'I want to see credentials, qualifications, certificates, the lot. This is my house and no one works here unless I say so.'

She's furious and I'm with her all the way. Keep hold of those keys, nurse, once you let them go it's bloody hard to pick them up again. Does your CV say 'Care Giver', 'Keeper of the Keys?' And does mine say 'Looked After', 'Cared For?' Don't take your keys for granted, shrugging and smiling behind her back.

It's angry too. You can tell in the way that he masturbates. I've never thought about it before but it is possible to masturbate angrily. I have time to list a hundred ways in which it is possible to masturbate, a hundred adverbs. Tenderly, tentatively, hungrily, sadly, cheerily, messily, repetitively, seriously, flippantly, clumsily … He's still at it. It's exhausting, and I'm only standing still. He's throwing himself physically, vocally, mentally, emotionally, into the business as if it is his life's work. Will it be worse if I run and cover my head in the blanket? Will the part of the sound that is lost continue in my ears? This is not a situation I have planned for. It seems so startling and so predictable, that whilst she sorts the sheets into unfathomable piles and checks her handbag again in the mirror, he should be doing this. It has, after all, to be done. The lunch trolley's coming. The little picnic that is taken sometimes in silence and sometimes in rage. He is still at it. This man has really got something

150

here and I'm the only person who's honoured to witness it. I'll have to risk getting stuck with that lost bit of sound.

'Could you wait for your turn?'

In the fluster of the moment I'm too eager and I'm right up against the gloop before my name is called. She's been here eight months and she's so docile I have to be angry for her. Eight months. How do you do it? I can't do eight minutes without my head turning circles and travelling years. But here's the clue. Watch. So calm, serene, unwrapping the slices, laying them on the roll. She knew she'd been here eight months. I asked, and she told me straight away, with no pause while her eyes flicked up to count.

Stolen time, lost time, time vandalised and raped by mental illness. Whole chunks of whole lives until the only answer left seems to be to live whilst you're here, in some form very different to that which you know.

The vagueness drifts through me like a ghost but I can't begin to define.

Romy Wood

ECT

ECT has a reputation for being an unpleasant procedure to receive and to observe being delivered, though I am not one of those who demonise it. People I knew who received it complained sometimes of a nasty headache and also of temporary memory loss, but they insisted that they felt 'brighter' and more self-confident.

Of course, with muscle relaxant and anaesthetic delivered beforehand it is nowadays modified and safer. The modern procedure is quite subdued. Sometimes it is difficult to know whether a seizure has actually occurred.

Earlier deliveries of this procedure were very different and often resulted in violent seizures which caused injuries and were difficult for staff to control.

There was a long-stay patient of late middle age who had experienced such an episode years before I met him. So intense was his seizure that he had actually broken one of his legs. This wasn't noticed at the time, so the fracture fused out of place, resulting in one leg being shorter than the other by several inches. He had to wear a reinforced boot for the rest of his life.

I used to wonder whether, as this man was virtually mute and lost in his schizophrenia, and as he seemed oblivious to the reason for his limp, and as he had no one to act on his behalf, then the fuss that would accompany such a matter today was unlikely to occur then because of the harsher, simple, and fatalistic attitudes that then prevailed.

Keith Sullivan

Big, Daunting, Edwardian, Outdated

When I was growing up the familiar taunt, when your behaviour was odd or outlandish, was that you would 'go to Whitchurch'. I did not believe that fifteen years later that I would indeed go to Whitchurch. I was transferred there from another hospital. It was Christmas time. The Christmas decorations seemed incongruous and out of place. There was a competition between the wards as to who could have the best Christmas decorations. On my ward were huge, bizarre penguins. Their surreal nature seemed to negate any serious feelings of unhappiness temporarily and then just grated on my senses.

My Great-Aunt Bess spent her life in Whitchurch and growing up I was following in her footsteps.

Anonymous

Crisis Recovery

I sat in this one particular armchair and remained there for the best part of three days. As I sat, I kept looking along the passage thinking all I have to do is reach the end, out through the door, and then I'd be free. Why didn't I do it? I was too shaky to stand, so weak. Many inpatients approached me. But I was so withdrawn, one by one they would all say 'I understand just exactly how you're feeling, I was exactly the same three weeks ago and the first three days are always the worst. We'll speak when you feel your feet start on the road to recovery.' They couldn't be more correct. Within five days, I felt ready to communicate with the other inmates. All from completely different walks of life, most were there for different addictions and reasons.

There were those who were genuine causes, with realisations of their needs. Those who treated it as a break with no intention of not drinking again. They were using the ward for rest, food, a bed, and the medication they needed to stop any side effects they would have received if they had not had these tablets. Oh, and they also had a chance of using a shower and bath. The perfect answer. Others were genuine in their quest of a cure, to live, not just exist, which is what happens when you're under the influence of alcohol or drugs. You really do just exist.

My stay on the ward had its reward, was successful, but the hardest task was on leaving the ward. That's when the reality of being able to contact the people who still dealt in Class A drugs hit home, and the availability of alcohol. Name a shop where you're unable to purchase some. Not in chemists, butchers, charity chops, clothes shops, but they are so few in comparison to pubs in abundance, Spar, newsagents.

Kathryn Alison Griffiths

Mystery Yacht

From the mid 1970s, for about thirteen years, an eighteen-foot fixed-keel yacht, supported by a wheeled cradle, was parked on the hospital track that passed the old stable yard of Velindre Grange. The metal mast was folded back on to the tarpaulin covering the deck.

Staff got so used to passing back and fore that they simply forgot about it. It was just never mentioned. No one seemed to find it unusual that such a large and valuable object was left unattended.

As the years went by, leaves and debris began to pile up on the vessel and the cradle tyres became deflated.

It seems that Whitchurch staff always presumed that it was owned by someone in Velindre Hospital or the Grange and Velindre staff presumed the opposite. Eventually, an official letter was sent around the hospitals in the late 1980s, asking the owner of the yacht to remove it. Nobody replied because nobody 'on site' owned it.

It remained for a short while in what, by then, was an obviously abandoned state until, one night, it simply disappeared. I never discovered its fate.

Keith Sullivan

Signs

'No dog walking.' The sign was direct and blunt in its instruction. Below it, a small, scruffy Jack Russell terrier was enthusiastically scuffing up grass, in the way dogs do, watched indulgently by an elderly gent in a trilby who was holding its lead. He noticed me watching as I drove slowly past, looking for the entrance to the car park (which wasn't signposted), and raised his hat in a manner which, although polite, suggested I should mind my own business and let the dog take care of his.

It was my first visit to Whitchurch Hospital and my first experience of the complete disregard in which most signs were held. No smoking signs seemed to serve only to remind people that they needed a cigarette. No parking, an invitation to leave your vehicle directly beneath. 'Fire alarm – Break glass', however, was often interpreted as an instruction, resulting in many false alarms; and much rushing to windows for impressionable female staff fortunate enough to work in the offices surrounding the goods yard, where the fire engine pulled up and swarms of burly young firemen leapt into action.

I didn't know any of this on that particular morning. I had passed the hospital gates, with their imposing Victorian columns, many times, but never really taken any notice of what lay beyond. Today, however, I had an interview. 'HR Assistant, 18½ hrs per week, hours flexible' had caught my eye in the *Western Mail*. I wasn't really looking for a new job but I still had the old Personnel habit of buying a local paper on the days recruitment ads appear.

I looked around me as I continued along the path. Horse chestnut trees were dotted here and there, dropping spiky-cased conkers which squeaked and crunched under unwary feet on the path. I couldn't resist picking up one or two which had split, exposing their shiny brown contents – the children would love these – and slipping them into my handbag. I looked around guiltily. I realised I was being watched. A small, wiry woman of indeterminate age, wearing a long camel-coloured coat and a brown knitted hat, was sitting on a low wall at the edge of the path on the other side of the road.

'Got a fag, love?' she croaked in a loud bass voice, startling from such a small frame.

'Sorry, I don't smoke,' I managed to answer through my embarrassment, and feeling I needed to offer an explanation for my stooping behaviour, 'I've just been collecting conkers … For my daughters …'

She continued staring at me.

'Got a fag?' she asked again in a less hopeful tone.

'Sorry.'

I shook my head and smiled apologetically. She turned her head away towards the gates, presumably looking for any other passers by who may be able to oblige.

'Morning, Matron,' I heard her bellow to no one in particular as I continued along the path to my interview. I crossed the road and looked for the way in to the hospital. Two steep steps led to the main entrance – a set of modest double doors which seemed a bit out of keeping with the overall grandeur of the front of the building. I pushed the left hand door (more signs – 'turn handle and push') and found myself in a large, dark, and shabby hallway, gloomy corridors stretching off at either side. A mahogany reception desk with tarnished brass rails sprawled on my right, an old-fashioned push bell at the front with a tattered, much-sellotaped sign – 'Please ring for attention'. But I didn't need to; my letter had given me directions.

Through the double doors, the main corridor seemed like another world after the gloom of the hallway. Sunlight streamed in through a series of high windows on the right; brass plaques lined the wall on my left, bearing legends such as 'The Shannon Bed, endowed 1917'. My footsteps echoed along the empty corridor and I tried to imagine what it would be like to work here.

Little did I know then that I was to spend the next ten years finding out!

Sian Thomas

History Snapshots – 5

Throughout the 1920s, under the enlightened and pioneering leadership of Dr Edwin Goodall, as far as the number of patients being discharged back into society – rather than being incarcerated for life – was concerned, Whitchurch Hospital compared more than favourably with any mental hospital in the country.

Goodall had given the hospital a great start and in 1929 he was succeeded by Dr Peter McCowan, a far-thinking and insightful man who was both a doctor and a barrister.

Dr McCowan believed in the individuality of the patient and was well aware of the danger of institutionalizing people with mental health problems. He introduced a parole system at Whitchurch, short leaves of absence for patients, and several 'open door' wards. Individual lockers were now provided in the wards and institutional garments, previously made in the hospital sewing room, disappeared to be replaced by the patients' own clothes.

Occupational therapy was introduced in April 1930, creating an ethos within the establishment where all patients were encouraged, through an organised and effective programme of creative activity, to get in touch with reality. The hospital's first psychiatric social worker was appointed the following year.

Treatment in the 1930s still consisted of procedures such as hydrotherapy and continual bath treatment, sulphur therapy, and even electrotherapy. But under Dr McCowan's benevolent regime there was extra emphasis on the individual. Only in extreme cases was individual freedom to be curtailed or limited.

The Mental Health Act of 1930 was the harbinger of change for mental health services and during the next ten years much progress was made in areas such as treatment and research. Voluntary admissions and discharges to and from hospitals like Whitchurch, essential in the building of trust between patients and doctors, were especially important.

In particular, however, during the 1930s there was, finally, some movement in the attitude of the general public to mental health and mental illness. For the first time people began to see that mental illness was not something to be ashamed of or hidden away. It was an illness, just like TB, cancer, or measles, and could be treated or helped. Such attitudes were not universal but it was a start.

Dr McCowan resigned his post at Whitchurch in 1937, being succeeded by Dr Thomas J Hennelly. He came at a difficult time as just two years later Britain was plunged, once more, into a long and brutal war. Whitchurch was again pressed into use as a military hospital, the 800 beds that were provided making Whitchurch the largest emergency services hospital in Wales. Over the next six years British, American, and, occasionally, German soldiers were regularly admitted to the hospital wards.

This time, however, mentally ill patients were not spirited away to other hospitals. Whitchurch continued its work as a mental hospital, albeit on a much reduced scale and size, and when peace returned in 1945 it was ready to resume its normal duties. But within a few years, new legislation and government thinking had turned the world of Whitchurch Hospital upside down.

Phil Carradice
Author, historian and lead writer on The Whitchurch Project

Jigsaw

Every mind in the room spins in a separate universe. She
cries, all the time, because it's her fault and her aunty says
Jesus loves her. He smiles; no one speaks to you in here.
He's so lucid, you can see it even through the smoke. She
looks like a librarian and she calls you spawn of Satan.
And the whole room shuffles like a great live jigsaw, the
pieces coated in grime and the sounds filtered through
antique gauze.

Door wedged open and she sits with the chair against it,
keeping watch, flicking the pages of celebrities, yawning
while the figure on the bed twitches.

Walk up the little corridor and back. Push the door, sit,
stand, up and back. And the thick red door to the steps is
locked, triple-locked, staring out at the bins and some grey
shingle, it would be good to be out there. The window
from the dayroom shows and endless sunshine garden and
a groundsman free to dig.

Romy Wood

I am trying to pinpoint what I do not like about Whitchurch Hospital ... and when you find out it's curtains!!!

I went outside.
It was a sunny day ... not cold at all.
But there was nowhere to lie down...
The grass was immaculately mown...
like the green baize of a snooker table.
But even this ... I could not lie down on it
to rest.
I'm trying to imagine what was the matter.
with the external   as if maybe I needed
a piece of linoleum   yes to stop the damp
of the grass being absorbed into my clothes
as I lay horizontally...
enjoying the sunshine   alone   alone   alone
in front of the main building.

Anthos Polycarpou

164

I know i'm bloody crazy
I know i'm bloody mad
and when i'm schizophrenic
the things i do seem bad
but when i come through it
you know i do feel sad
for causing you to fret
over my trite fad

you see i get so manic
right inside the dream
acting out the basis
of some stark primordial scene

Roger Gilbert

Written August 1991

On the Receiving End:
a twenty-first century experience

Whitchurch Hospital 2004-06 is a place where apparently the staff receive therapy, but the patients do not. 'Therapy' is a word never mentioned and is probably still the case as far as inmates are concerned.

A strict regime dominates, 'treatment' following a purely medical model with a culture for those unlucky enough to have to seek help there, is one of being 'done-to' rather than empowered to return to recovery even in this, the twenty-first century.

Inpatients at the hospital, even those who are not sectioned, are confined to one of the 'locked wards' and at all times have to seek permission to leave them. The nursing staff rarely, talk *with* their patients in any meaningful way but rather *at* them as though fearful of some type of cross-contamination or with any sense of compassion often remaining locked inside the ward office and so unavailable for much of the time.

Time drags on these wards where there is nothing to do but watch television, to play pool, or take part in so-called OT which in reality was playing Bingo or listening to CDs. The whole setup was surreal and a travesty of twenty-first century mental health care.

A Dickensian culture of 'them and us' predominates in this nineteenth-century environment. It is one of long, endless corridors and dank wards smelling largely of stale cigarette smoke. The clinical relationship is one of confrontation, and an aggressive one where physical restraints are commonly practised as I myself saw when a woman patient was forced to the ground in a corridor of the hospital by four male nurses while being admitted and forcibly injected by a female nurse.

However one of the most terrifying as well as humiliating experience for many every week was The Ward Round.

Here the patient is summoned into the presence of The Consultant. This is reminiscent of a mini Star Chamber where patients are cross-examined by 'the expert in mental health' with a team of at least five or six hangers-on while also being exhibited to curious trainee students within the confines of a small room measuring not more than ten by eight feet. They are as though on trial for some serious offence and not for seeking help, nevertheless a patient can be accused of not 'responding to treatment' and so the medication is to be increased – no questions asked; no second opinion to be given.

It is within the power of such a gentleman – it is usually an older male clinician – to retain a person, or to 'section' them for long periods of time, sometimes even by a doctor whose grasp of the English Language is basic, not with first language skills at times can barely be understood yet nevertheless is given life-altering powers over those unfortunate enough to be admitted to the, 'care' of this place.

The operating regime is more akin to that of a prison than a hospital environment where the dank environment with minimal washing facilities, less updated than in a prison environment, and often in many cases in an unhygienic state with toilets left dirty, and with bathroom floors unwashed, left smelling of urine often together with cigarette butts littering these areas.

Patients were left to smoke openly on their beds in the mixed dormitory wards, and shared by up to twenty-five people – both men and women, and where the only privacy were badly hung curtains around these bed closets with women patients having to walk past the male beds to get to their own sleeping 'space', but with no partition or privacy existing between the two. No Health & Safety Regulations in evidence here, but after all it's only for housing the mentally ill.

Despite many protestations on the walls that inmates will be treated with 'dignity and respect' and so flippantly and publicly bandied around by the mental health management as though it in fact existed, a culture of implicit 'blame' pre-dominates as though it is through some personal moral failure that one has ended up here seeking the, 'treatment' as doled here out by the Welsh NHS, rather than through the pressures of traumatic life events.

Time can drag endlessly on these wards, punctuated only by the arrival of an ancient tea trolley at regular intervals and the piercing shriek of the fire alarm system that is centrally controlled so it can go off at any time including 4 a.m. in the morning, lasting for not seconds, but many minutes as it is not able to be switched off manually, constituting an added type of auditory torture to the patients – day and night: a season in hell.

De-humanised, forgotten, and lingering in an airless dayroom – whose windows can never be opened – the monotony only punctuated at intervals by meals arriving from a faraway kitchen within the bowels of the hospital and brought in by trolleys – lukewarm on arrival, and with even the staff not knowing what the food they were serving was meant to be. Fruit and salads were unknown here except on occasions for perhaps three bananas and two oranges to be given on a ward of at least fifteen patients. Staff of course did not share such, 'food', but brought in their own.

Staff, often with their sadistic tendencies unbridled

here, keys jangling from their belts like prison, patrol the wards, often bullying patients some being strip-searched and accused of not having taken their medication, or forced into taking medication on an empty stomach.

At Whitchurch Hospital, in my experience, sadly very little had changed in the attitude towards those who suffer mental distress since the novel, *Over Flew Over the Cuckoo's Nest* was written in the 1950s.

One lasting image left with me is of a pale face desperately pressed up against a window of a locked ward as I was led down a corridor, and the far off sound of a person screaming, but never stopping.

Each night at dusk huge flocks of crows and jackdaws would congregate in the giant horse chestnut trees of the grounds, all cawing like harbingers on the edge of doom; very much like the black crow observed by the poet Sylvia Plath.

Somehow I survived. Others I know have not.

Note: In 2007-09 plans were well advanced for a new state-of-the-art unit to be built in the grounds of the hospital, together with a new ethos in place: to date nothing has happened yet with millions already spent plans have now been shelved: mental health in Wales continuing to remain very much a Cinderella Service.

G. K. Brightmore

All These Things I Want to Do

I didn't take any notice of where we were going until we got to Whitchurch Hospital. I said that I knew where we were. 'How do you know Whitchurch Hospital?' they asked.

I replied that my mum had been there, although it was my sister that I had visited.

We went to the assessment room – there was a female police officer and two other male officers. The room was dark and small.

I got very upset. 'I have all these things I want to do.' 'You still can,' the female officer said.

But in my head I knew that this wasn't going to be over in just a couple of months.

You know in the same way that cancer can run in the same family. I saw my mum go through something that I knew I didn't want to go through myself. It was the worst thing that could happen to me.

People don't respect you if you've been to a hospital like Whitchurch. It's easier if you've gone to prison. It was like a prison, or like a concentration camp, like in *Schindler's List* – with the smoke coming out of the tower.

There was a darkness to the place – an old building.

It felt like the end of the world – I was not going to be able to do what I wanted to do.

It was a cold, wet day, the day I went in, a depressing day, must've been around October.

I was frightened about what was going to happen – not knowing – it was a different experience going in as a patient, decisions are being made about your body, tablets, your control is taken away.

I wanted to go to college and I was worried about medical records.

Time was a big factor. I didn't want to waste time. Because my childhood was wasted – wasn't able to do exams, 'by the time this ends I'm going to be too old to do anything.'

Because of my childhood I had to be independent and in control – couldn't rely on my mum.

Now control was being taken away – it was frightening – I didn't even know these people – the staff – what kind of backgrounds and personalities they had.

I didn't want people to visit me – as few people to visit as possible, didn't even want my parents to visit, didn't want Dad to be upset again after seeing my mum and my sister go through the same experience.

I wanted to deal with it on my own, by myself. That's my way, the way I've learned to cope.

Whitchurch Hospital was only ever spoken about in a negative way – 'the worst place you could end up in'.

I didn't want to talk about it, I wanted to protect myself from bullying. Things were difficult enough at home, people talked – about my mum's behaviour in public.

I remember the first time I spoke to a headteacher about it, I was sixteen, I said that things were difficult at home. Before then, I never answered the question 'What do your parents do?' – I would avoid the question.

Anonymous

No More Battles

Up and down stalks the old man from Ward B15. His teeth are few, his speech has aged in the last two decades, and the words come out in chunks. He yells, 'Take shelter … Messerschmitts … coming!' and runs up and down the main corridor, his flies never buttoned to the top. By teatime, when the doors bite shut for the night, he can only mumble to the straggling visitors: 'You are going to die. The Germans are coming.'

Years ago, when he still had a name he could remember, he forced frightened patients into dark cupboards, threatened them with brooms that to him were rifles, wore a battered metal bucket as a helmet. He no longer seeks the enemy, but the staff banned him from shouting air raid warnings in the dayroom. He is locked in the past, has nowhere to go. His is a world where feet walk on crumbling lino that smells of Jeyes disinfectant and wasted years.

There is no water in the trenches, so he cannot wash. Forcing him into a bath is a three-nurse operation, never attempted on the day a new patient is admitted. Once, his screams drove a poor soul in search of Jesus he thought lived beyond the glass of the newly built verandah. The poor devil bled to death.

He has a weakness for custard. He plays with the lumps, squashes them flat on the side of his pudding bowl, then rushes back to his lonely battlefield. His daughter no longer visits him. She threw away his Victoria Cross, moved to another town, left no forwarding address.

He was handsome once, kind, and the bravest of all.

172

That is what it said, in the newspaper her mother kept in her underwear drawer during all those years of hoping. She died ten years ago. When George stood by her grave he asked whose funeral it was. Did not remember her name.

Claudia Rapport

Detox

I have suffered from panic attacks and acute anxiety disorder since I was eighteen. After a few years of hell I realized that alcohol seemed to calm me down but this was the start of a slippery slope.

After almost six years of drinking heavily I was admitted to Whitchurch for my first detox. I was amazed at the care and attention they put into looking after people in my situation and after the two-week detox I felt so much better and was even able to work for the first time, but this didn't last long and the panic attacks started to come back. So did the drinking.

Due to the mess I was now making I found myself with the Salvation Army, who also tried to help, but living in a hostel situation such as the Salvation Army provided made things worse. I was admitted to Whitchurch for the second time at age twenty-nine. Due to the lack of space and government funding I only had three days' treatment which was amazing but to then go back to a hostel was no good.

So now I find myself waiting again for another detox on the Adfer wing. This time for two weeks. To be able to return to a safe location afterwards with continued help and the right medication to help with the anxiety.

Will Miller

Picture

There's a blank space on the wall where a picture used to be. And that's where they are, it's ideal. The frame shape draws you in so they can get your full attention. How brazen that it's opposite the window. They know they can't be seen. We used to close the curtains – they're laughing a little – as if. You're smothered by stark light, crushed coffee cups and soggy fag butts. Decades – old air in an antique room. The particles shift very, very slowly, shunted by your entrance. You begin to stagnate. Your lungs fall into step. You keep your suitcase close but you forgot your passport and now it's out of reach.

On reception, they're ignoring a telephone. In the consulting room, they're rumbling and writing on a carbon sheet. Referred by: out-of-hours. Time: 1:30 a.m. No passport. The telephone gives up. The doctor coughs. The picture yawns.

This room is the winging lid of the bin where grime collects and thuds soundlessly to the bottom. Even the stench isn't too bad if you keep a distance. 'Could you join us through here again … Put your clothes on, please. Thank you.' The room sighs suddenly, it doesn't want to let you go. Only the doctor's eyes make you stand, take hold of your suitcase, wade through the dank fog when it would be so much easier to lie still. Let them stay in the picture and yawn while you fuse gently with the carpet.

Romy Wood

Early Embarrassment

Coming from a Chapel background, hence then quite conservative in my attitudes, I remember my first experience of a nude lady. Shortly after starting work at the hospital, I was sent down to a female ward to help out with a patient who had become very upset and required medication via an intramuscular injection. As I walked through the ward door, I heard swearing and there, in a side room, was a lady, naked, lying face down on a bed, shouting loudly and surrounded by female nurses. All I could see was her buttocks. The sister requested me to help hold her. I didn't know where to hold her or what to do. I was too embarrassed. So, I held her ankle with my finger and thumb and averted my eyes while a female nurse gave her her intramuscular medication in the exposed buttock. Afterwards, the sister looked at me with disdain and remarked that I 'had not been much bloody help', as I left, still embarrassed and puzzled about what had happened.

My first experience of naked bodies in the hospital.

Anonymous

The Harvey Jones Unit

I spent time at the Harvey Jones as a student in 1991; it had been a therapeutic community but by then it had lost much of its magic. Part of its 'specialness' was the fact that it was a place where people could come and talk about feelings, a therapeutic community. But this was in the main a bit of a myth. It had lots of meetings, therapeutic drama groups, etc. but, at the same time, it couldn't control the kids.

Things were changing. The therapeutic community was becoming history. What was needed was a hospital for kids with severe mental health problems – at least as far as the trusts, politicians, etc. were concerned.

The building was in terrible condition – it was neglected, partly because its future was uncertain. Its death was never really planned – it was uncertain. So there was no investment.

It was heavily institutionalised. Rules were paramount. Staff didn't see challenge to rules as opportunity for growth. The nurses, the medics, the therapists – all working separately. The nurses really had control. *One Flew Over the Cuckoo's Nest*? – that was what it was like. The system had to work and it destroyed people's ability and inclination to change things.

The therapeutic element had been low – at times the place was useful, even helpful and supportive, but there was a dark side too.

The old H. Jones was on the site of Whitchurch psychiatric unit – you're actually starting people on a psychiatric career. You can move and change people but for some their psychosis (which was never treated in the early days, just not recognised) was so severe that they needed to be in a hospital.

As an adolescent unit nobody wants you – it's an impossible job. You can't do what people want you to do – the problem isn't just the kid. Kids kick off; they're expensive; behaviour remains a problem. We demonise adolescence and in the health services we demonise adolescence services.

Steve Killick

Impressions

My first impressions of Whitchurch Hospital were from a child's point of view. I believe I was the youngest patient they had had there. It was not long after the Second World War. At the time there were still people who were very mentally ill and were in the process of being transferred to Bridgend Park Hospital. The grounds were surrounded by strong metal fencing and there were huge iron gates to the front. The lovely church was in use for Sunday services and there were piggeries and allotments. The hospital was self-sufficient, having its own laundry and kitchens. Every door was automatically locked behind you and there were locked side-rooms. Every ward had a coal fire and the coal was kept in a large cupboard outside each ward. The beds were metal and everything, even the paintwork, was very dark and drab. There was a large hall with a stage where dances were held and staff put on shows.

When I was ill the doctor suggested to my mother that as I was usually worse at night, perhaps I could go and stay in. My mother cried as the stigma of Old Whitchurch Hospital was bad. Nevertheless I went in. I put on a stone in weight through eating the food and was thoroughly spoiled by the staff.

Ann Cummings Teear

HQ

It is sometimes referred to by a friend who has also been there as 'HQ'. There is obviously still a stigma associated with the place but for those involved it's a kind of central building.

The building itself, particularly in winter, can appear gloomy and depressing, especially with the long corridors. Outsiders, especially family, tend to notice this more but for some reason, as a patient there, I don't think you necessarily look at it as being a depressing building. Often your mind is so taken up with other things that you don't really notice the surroundings.

It is generally a place you don't want to have to go and when you are there, you're always thinking about when you'll be getting out. Yet it can still be a good place to be at times. It can be quite boring if you're stuck on the ward but most of the time other people are friendly which always helps.

Nick Fisk

The Push

Being human is not a crime
Having an addiction is not a crime
Asking for help is not a crime
No more secrets, no more lies
A bridge too far or one step at a time
A future with a clear mind
At the end of the day
it's your life
YOU DECIDE

Will Miller

Past Tense

He doesn't even realise he's done it, I don't think; doesn't
realise that one question has provoked such a response.
My reaction is internalised, which is good, as it means that
I can control my feelings, or at least how they appear on
the surface, even from those trained to spot such things. I
am sat in his office, the first meeting of what I think is
meant to be many. We start off talking about my attitudes,
likes, dislikes, about my problems adjusting to situations. I
don't know what he has in mind when he asks me it,
though, just one of those traditional questions head-doctors
ask of patients, running through the roles that we have to
play, our conversation pre-scripted. He has to ask, I have
to respond the way I do. It's a difficult feeling to describe,
like something has been switched on, a barely contained
explosion that propels me forwards – that's why they're
called triggers, I suppose – and it's like at that moment
there is nothing in me but edges. Even years later, the
closest I can get is to refer to a film, yet another second-
hand account, another sense of dislocation and distance.
I'm in *Blade Runner* – an unfortunately apt title – and it's
the opening scene. I am Leon, he is Holden. He asks the
question and it's the trigger I don't even realise existed
until that point. He doesn't see what he's done – his notes
reveal that – and the letters chasing me for a follow-up
peter out. We don't meet again. Do I blame him? Yes,
even now. My dislike of questions designed to elicit an
emotional response, especially one that is then not
observed, is still sharp. Looking back, I realise that he may
have been right, and that he took the brunt of my

transference, but that doesn't matter. More than fifteen years later I still come back here and feel it all over again, and I don't want to have to. I am always here, somewhere. It's not his fault, I was here before he ever arrived.

Nic Tate

Occupational Therapy

A nurse would come and say which classes or occupational therapies were on for that day and another queue formed. Some were capable of making their own way there, others had to be taken and counted. Unlock the ward door and off down the corridor. High, wide, with bands along the walls of half brick and paint. The floors were shiny and buffed. Polish and Windolene coated you on your trek. Still the heat.

Today they are making trays and baskets from cane. There is a tinge of the Orient handling the cane. It was very long and had to be soaked in water to handle. The old hands were very adept at making the trays. Using brightly coloured beads near the handle part. Some were sold and some you could buy. I can remember making a little cat basket and a stuffed toy cat which I gave to my sister Pat. She had it for years. Everything was tactile, the jewel-coloured felts had a scent to them also the kapok used for stuffing. It reminded me of the sewing my mother did at home. She had a straw basket for her needles and pins and the lid was filled with kapok. I used to sit and look through the hundreds of buttons which she kept there.

Where we sat for our meals the tables had very heavy chenille clothes and there were palm-type trees in big china vases, and aspidistras. Very Victorian.

Ann Cummings Teear

To Be Discontinued

After Whitchurch, 18th November 1993

We didn't get very far, you and I, circling
through the recalcitrant hour on a surfeit

of thin ice. The going good to firm until
that question about grounds, then we were

talking with feet, the answer in a patellar
reflex and digging in of heels. The return

home never came, for years words pounding
the pavement as I never stopped running

from the rhythm of that line. It was all legs
when it should have been ears,

but we never listened, you and I, between
my feet and your assumptions a chasm

of metres no words could traverse. Lines
never meeting, mouths walking in opposite

directions, case closed after the slip
of an EEG and absence, though there's no

closure to *who do you blame for your anger?*
Fear of the then unknown and unnoted

transference behind in all the wrong ways,
I left with the sharp wit and swallowed rage

I ground into my soles and have walked
over since. There is still enough blame to

throw about; you and yours, true, but me
and mine too – mostly me, as I am only now

learning to live in the length of my body.

Nic Tate

Disappearances

There was a room, known by its internal telephone number – 247. It was a nurse-management office, full of beautiful furniture including a huge mahogany desk and a bookcase with leaded glass panels. (One of a handful of richly endowed rooms that had hardly changed since the hospital had opened.)

In the late 1980s these Edwardian pieces started to disappear. It seemed impossible at the time to discover what had happened to them. Were they still in the building? Had they been moved to another room/another building? And why?

There used to be elaborate brass coat/hat hangers on the inside face of the door of Room 247. One weekend during this period of disappearances these valuable hangers were removed – probably the first time they had left their position. Was it theft? Or were they set up elsewhere in the hospital or its scattered units in order to please someone?

At about the same time, *all* of the even more elaborate coat hangers, about fifteen in number, mounted outside the board room were unscrewed and removed. This blatant theft of irreplaceable items made people sit up and take notice. Security began to be tightened.

The disappearance that annoyed me the most was the removal of a beautiful wall barometer from its position in the front hall. This occurred one Saturday night while a group of members of the public were waiting, at the front hall, for taxis to take them home, following a function in the main hall.

The barometer had been the gift (in gratitude) of a

distinguished, local, and well-known family.

One evening, in the early 1980s, I arrived to work night duty. The night office was buzzing with conversation around one subject: the disappearance of a giant roll of carpet from a secure storeroom (actually an unused ward). We were instructed to keep a special watch and increase our security vigil. A senior colleague and I checked the store via an observation window, sometime during the early hours and found everything locked and secure. The rolled-up companion of the missing carpet was safe but I was astonished at its bulk. It was huge – industrial sized and about 4 feet in diameter. Much equipment and many men would have been needed to move it. We began to wonder whether the missing carpet had ever arrived in the first place, especially when we realised that there was no damage to doors or windows.

During the early 1960s, staff using the nurses' dining room were served at nicely laid tables by waitresses. Some, though not all, of the salt and pepper pot sets were of silver and were mounted with enamelled badges baring the city of Cardiff coat of arms. They had been used there since the place was opened. They had to be withdrawn in the late 60s because some of them disappeared. It was a part of a changing attitude in society which, of course, infiltrated the hospital.

Keith Sullivan

Cocktails in Babylon

Scene: Cardiff Hospital, 2004 - 2006.

This prose-poem was 'triggered', but not inspired by what I witnessed of the mental distress and it's so called, 'treatment' by NHS Wales.

Also by Kit Wright's haunting poem, 'The Dayroom' making me feel it was necessary to give some, 'voice' myself to what I witnessed especially now 2014, and in light of NHS cuts to Welsh Health Services.

The radio in my head is playing over and over – can this be, 'The Final Countdown'?

Our, 'windows of perception' are clouded, and chemically adulterated here in this suburban, 'asylum' that could stand in for – Abu Grad.

The Doctor appears to be a D.J. wearing a dirty pullover, speaks broken English taking down our medical histories, but never making eye contact here on the, Acute Unit – 2004.

The morning Drug Trolley snakes down a greasy, green linoleum corridor then stops to be guarded by nurses, as though fearing an assault ready to discharge its lethal contents down our throats: it's time – time for the Meds.

The drugs appear to be brightly coloured *Smarties*, and yet in reality as dangerous as any Class A Drug given out in total silence, like a Litany on the edge of Doomsday.

But this is no Sweet Shop, the windows are iron-barred, the air is stale with nicotine hanging in yellow clouds in the sunless air together with the smell of last's night's meal with the reek of unwashed urine lingering together in the rotten air as we wait, like naughty children, to be comatosed – medicated to within an inch of our reason obediently forced to submit to these, 'experts' in the field of Mental Health being 'done-to' but never empowered – waiting in a line under harsh strip-lighting, meekly as lambs fearing, The Final Countdown will begin again or, 'deadly restraint' will be used; even ECT the treatment of choice – should we, 'not respond to treatment' being chemically coshed to numbness.

CLOSPAINE – EFFOXOR – METAZAPIN – OLANAZAPINE

The arsenal here is endless.

Night falls then yet again as the night time Drugs Trolley rolls in like some awful nemesis at 9.15 p.m. to 'deliver us from evil' abandoned here beyond the reach of hope: invisible in the acute with our psychiatric disorders, a drug for every spiritual malaise – no one here has yet heard of Freud, but neatly categorized as Clinical Depression – Bi-Polar – Schizophrenia – Borderline Personality Disorder, or if they run out of labels, 'Challenging Behaviour' will do.

So we must submit our minds to, 'Treatment', and our souls to whatever Mercy may exist in this Universe lingering in the Dayroom with the constant cries of a woman screaming, day and night behind a closed door that she be let out to go back to Tongwynlais as urgently as anyone could, but no one goes to comfort her. Compassion is not a necessary qualification here in the field of 'mental health'.

But the Radio in my head continues as I fear that 'The Final Countdown' will soon come as we all wait at the pleasure of the staff in the Dayroom like little Miss Fucking Sunshines left to sit on dirty plastic chairs now having been diagnosed, drugged and given our, 'Care Plans' that we are not allowed to read; so all should be well – should it not?

CRACKERS – LOONEY – BARKING – BONKERS – NUTTERS

We stare through grimy windows, abandoned in the Dayroom, 'Deliver us from Evil' and also the clutches of the delusional ward psychiatrist, a consultant who thinks he's standing in for God, or some other patriarchy. Yet outside I see the ancient chestnut trees 'sway' in magnificent sympathy for us, who can find no mercy here, stranded before the thirty-six-inch *Plasma TV Screen* screaming out at us it's victims, from morning until midnight in the Dayroom as yet another tea trolley rattles in, and stops as we scrabble for the tepid tea before the milk is used, and pouring it into heavy-duty, clipped cups afraid to ask for more, only for what is prescribed here in – Babylon …

RISPERAL – THORORAZINE – FLUOXETINE – TAMAMAZPAN

G. K. Brightmore

Who are you?

Halfway along the corridor leading from the hospital entrance to Tŷ Canol are four pencil drawings. They offer a welcome distraction, an invitation to pause on the journey down a neverending passageway. The pictures are well framed and hung in a neat row so you look at them in sequence. They show detailed drawings of everyday objects from the 1930s, but the items are arranged in interesting clusters that suggest they belonged to a busy person.

The first shows a sink plunger, an enamel mug, bar of Sunlight soap, and a piece of 'Kitts Blue' for whitening linens. The second shows a leather satchel open with its contents spilling out to reveal half a dozen glass marbles, a wooden-handled skipping rope, an apple, and a striped school tie. The third picture takes us back to the kitchen with a whistling kettle, an old-fashioned meat mincer just like my mother had clamped to the edge of a sturdy scrubbed pine table. Nearby is a set of weights neatly stacked in a pyramid, crowned at the top with a brass quarter ounce.

All are well drawn and intriguing but it is the fourth picture that demands my attention. Firstly a mechanical toy bear with a smiling expression, a candle stick with burnt down candle, a small oil lamp with a glass shade and screw mechanism for altering the wick. Nearby is a clock, large and functional but partially obscured by the other objects so it is impossible to tell if it is ten to eleven or five to ten. Above the clock there is a picture. A man in army uniform, sketched with precision, young, handsome, looking directly at me. As we stare at each other I feel unsettled. He holds my gaze until I am forced to speak. 'Who are you? Are you lost or found? Are you alive or dead? Missed or missing? Why are you here, in a picture within a picture? Are these your things?' He watches patiently as I speak, knowing but not sharing the answers.

My outburst over, we stare intently at each other once more, until he silently he bids me on my way.

Ruth Holgate

I Don't Belong Here

I first came here at Christmas. I remember little more than a sense of smug kindness at having visited a Parish member on a sacred family occasion. Seeing her take a sweet proffered by another patient and tuck it discreetly into a plant pot before begging us to take her with us. She was allowed to leave once she was better. I remember it was cold.

Today all is new and unfamiliar, that memory faded, as so many do, into a series of tiny snapshots. Blink. Blink. Gone. A smart wooden foyer gives way to cool pastel corridors. I stop at a window to lean my head against the glass. I am unwell. My notebook is held open, a shield against boundaries that threaten to blur. Outside, a 'sensory garden' is abandoned to the sun.

I tell myself that I do not belong here. Blink. Howling into the darkness and screaming her name (one of her names) my body a vessel for waves of pain which threaten to engulf me. Blink. My hand on hers slowly freezing as I repeat the 'Hail Mary' like a spell of protection. Gone.

Brass plaques give the names of those who have had beds donated in their honour. Further on posters encourage health and wellbeing. I read them all. In the canteen I sit like a drunk pretending to be sober, as the green walls and green tiles and green carpet sway around me. Welsh dragons abound.

I concentrate on a painting, *The Shrine* by John William Waterhouse. A dark-haired girl leans forward to smell a vase of pale flowers on a windowsill. Blink. Her hands rough with dirt after planting marigolds in the back garden. Blink. A pair of chunky green gardening shoes. Gone.

Opposite, someone is eating a baked potato with beans and cheese. Her favourite. I feel sick, and stand up to read the posters on the healthy eating display, pleased to see my choices are usually sensible.

I carry on my walk, one pastel shade after another broken up by mosaics and black and white photos. Blink. Her chuckles as she looks at a sepia image of a great aunt in owl-like glasses, her own hair in tight ringlets. Blink. A framed and faded smile. Gone.

Peering through a glass-panelled door I see a closed ward. Doors left open and light bulbs bare except for one, above which lingers half of a shattered lampshade. Vines have pushed through the windows and paper is scattered on the floor. It looks as though they left in a hurry.

In the corridor the wind has swept cigarette butts and litter into a comer. Graffiti adorns the walls. I lean my head against another window pane, outside a traffic cone is swamped by overgrown buddleias. A door is open. I walk outside. There was a time when I thought I would be safe here. No choices to make. No responsibility. Today though, I tell myself I don't belong here. I am glad I can choose to leave. Grief, like memory, will fade. Blink. Blink. Gone.

Rose Gleeson

Courtyard at West 5

The decaying limb of 'West 5' marks the end,
impending.
An absence of care perhaps,
or a mirror to the mind of all of us
who stand on the border looking out.
Or in.

The courtyard seems abandoned,
but notice the plants:
even left in the hands of chaos
the most neglected share a moment of clarity
once in a while.
Natural order emerges,
something *wants* to grow from this.

The plants are perfect – full of wellness.
They are doing what they were meant to,
they lack control, that's all.
There is nothing here to tame them,
only winter.
And even the darkest December day still has light and
spring will always begin again
to get the plants stirring.

Rebecca Parfitt

A Way of Life

Returning to the hospital after many years, what I expected to be unchanged was different, altered. Outside, some of the roads in the grounds were blocked off, pathways were overgrown, the buildings looked decayed, and like a lick of paint was needed. I was thinking of Shirley, knowing she still worked here. And then she appeared, going to work on Ward West One.

'It's dead, Steve, dead,' she said, 'I work with the old women, they've been here for years. It makes me grateful to have a home. But I wish I wasn't here, I'd rather be watching the rugby.' I asked her about what would happen when the ward closed. She said, 'Who knows? We're just waiting. Waiting to go.' I walk down and around the corridors with time to stop and stare. I never seemed to have the time to do that when I worked here. It's is like a whole world of which I only knew a part. Behind many doors were mysteries that just seemed to become invisible. There seemed to be ever-changing uses for a never-changing building. Signs for 'Clinical Governance' and 'Risk Management' printed on a piece of paper and stuck flimsily on doors suggested passing fashions and impermanence.

A poster spoke of 'Patient Stories for Service Improvement'. There must be so many stories waiting patiently to be told, from now and back a hundred years, from young and old, from people just passing through, from people, staff, and patients who spent their lives here. There must be stories of compassion and of cruelty, sometimes hard to tell each from the other. Others all too easy to distinguish.

Looking out the windows it seems nature is reclaiming its territory. Brambles and bushes filling the space, soon there will be trees, soon it will be all gone. Suddenly I feel enclosed, being inside one can only look out and even the open spaces are confined. There is a sense that once this was a safe place, secure, a sanctuary. A place for looking inside not wishing or wanting to look outside. It was away from life. But it became a way of life and it turned into a 'bin', a dustbin for rubbish. Now it's grown old and overgrown and outlived its usefulness even as that. It seemed to say 'not looked after.' As I judged it I wondered if it was also judging me, perhaps I'm also familiar but different and maybe a little overgrown. But maybe this hospital has also become too much like the people it tried to help and change; it's become the problem it was set up to solve.

Steve Killick

History Snapshots – 6

Under the terms of the new National Health Service Act, Cardiff City Mental Hospital was taken over by the Ministry of Health on 5th July 1948. The name Whitchurch Hospital was now formally adopted.

Whitchurch continued to have a high percentage of voluntary admissions, the terms of the 1959 Mental Health Act dispensing with the need for voluntary patients to give seventy-two hours' notice that they were intending to leave. According to one report by Dr Hennelly the Hospital had now achieved a recovery rate of 40%. Approximately 80% of the patients were discharged home or into the community, an amazingly high figure in a hospital with a residency that was regularly between six and seven hundred.

During the 1950s psychiatric treatments such as ECT and prefrontal leucotomy, even psychotherapy and prolonged narcosis, were largely replaced by psychotropic drugs. Many believe the use of these new drugs has been successful, others claim that their introduction merely subdued an individual's problems for a little while.

The number of medical and other staff at the hospital was greatly expanded during these years and, during the 1960s and 70s, a number of special units were established at the hospital, as alternatives to admission into the main building. Tegfan Day Hospital was opened in 1970, an earlier day hospital having been established in the 1950s. The Adfer Unit for people suffering from alcoholism and other addictions came into existence in 1964 and The Harvey Jones Unit for adolescents in 1973.

Other developments during these years included the Hafan Day Hospital, for elderly people with mental health problems, and the creation of a purpose-built Occupational Therapy Department, complete with gymnasium and various workshops.

In time, Dr Hennelly was succeeded by his deputy, Joseph Spillane, but by the end of the 1980s Whitchurch Hospital was already being seen by many as something of a dinosaur. It had been serving the community of Cardiff for almost eighty years and the buildings, clearly Victorian in design, were now out of date. In particular the hospital corridors – long, gloomy, and echoing – were far from conducive to the treatment of people with mental-health problems.

The All Wales Strategy, launched in 1983, had the avowed aim of producing a community-based mental health service and while Whitchurch Hospital remained in use, it was seen by many as a last-ditch resort where containment was more important than care and treatment. Whether or not that view was correct, it was still a far cry from the halcyon days of Dr Goodall.

In the early years of the twenty-first century, plans were made to close the old hospital with its echoing corridors and looming shadows, to sell off the original building, and provide more up-to-date facilities. The Harvey Jones Unit and Tegfan were demolished to make way for a new and much smaller residential unit while specialised provision at nearby Llandough Hospital and community-based support was also going to be offered. Financial restrictions prevented the full implementation of the plan and, for the moment at least, Whitchurch Hospital survives, although in a much restricted and reduced form.

Patient services are due to transfer to the University Hospital, Llandough in 2015/16. In due course, the site at Whitchurch, Northern Meadows as it is known, will be placed on the open market and will probably be developed *for housing. Existing buildings on the site will be redeveloped for mixed residential and commercial use.*

The substantial playing fields, where rugby, cricket, and bowls have been played for many years, will be protected and transferred to the ownership of the Council. Interestingly, there are several areas around the periphery of the site that have been earmarked as a wildlife corridor.

Even at the end of its active life the Whitchurch site still has a role to play.

Phil Carradice
Author, historian and lead writer on The Whitchurch Project

Who Cared?

A passage where a moth, trapped
against a cobwebbed window,
is witness to a padlocked
ward now cast aside.
Scents of mildewed words,
wanton eyes and musty
memories seep
under its door.
A cracked pane peers
down on a courtyard
freed from a gardener's fingers;
a tumult of buddleia
rusty briar, reckless nettles
thrusting saplings
trussed with bindweed.

Elizabeth Jones

Extract

… round convex mirrors high on the walls very near the ceiling, watching me, following my every move … the mirror seems to see things happen before they do … their presence prevents some things from happening but not everything.

Paula Windust

An education in Whitchurch Psychiatric 'Hospital' Adolescent Unit

I worked as a teacher in Whitchurch Psychiatric 'Hospital' Adolescent Unit for a short spell in the 1990s. I taught about fifteen pupils, of both sexes, aged between ten and sixteen years. The teaching room was a silent space enclosed by cold blue sky reaching walls. One wall carried a large closed window divided into panes, like the ones in Cardiff jail. The walls lacked the expected posters, maps, tables, and examples of pupils' work. The air was conditioned with the odour of sweat, cheap cleaning products, an oppressive heat, and a dust of terror.

The blank-faced pupils appeared light headed, light in weight and lacking in purpose. Like astronauts, the young people floated rather than walked. The teenagers seemed tired, sleepy, and ready for bed rather than eager to work, energetic, lively, loud, and full of fun and mischief expected of teenagers during the school day. Two young women looked like inhabitants of a war-torn country long hit by drought.

Discipline was not a problem in Whitchurch Psychiatric Hospital Adolescent Unit but staying awake was difficult for the pupils. Many a young person dozed off when attempting mathematics, comprehension, or art work. The pupils voiced no queries, questions, or comments.

The school day ended after the class met with a psychologist. For the last session everyone trooped into a bare walled hall-sized room with a frill of pastel armchairs. The teenagers collapsed into the furniture. The psychologist entered. The psychologist enquired about the young people's feelings in relation to the day's routine matters. Feelings? The only feeling the expressionless-faced pupils exhibited was that of exhaustion. The pupils' responses to the questions were words that might have had significance but they were not answers to the asked questions.

Were the pupils in pain? Did they know why they were in Whitchurch Psychiatric Hospital? I wondered what would be the long-term effect of being labelled mentally ill on the relationships, employment opportunities, and financial well-being on each of the young people.

On 29th April 2007, I woke to hear Radio 4's John Humphreys interview Teresa Cooper from Kent. Ms Cooper was bringing to the public's attention that psychotropic drugs, the type used in psychiatric 'hospitals', and other poisons labelled medicine, forced into her and other young women when they were in a care home, had resulted in their children having birth defects. Jeffery Aronson, Professor of Clinical Pharmacology at Oxford University stated, 'Changes in genes and chromosomes induced by drugs may lead to birth defects or abnormalities later in life.' I thought about the young people I taught in Whitchurch Psychiatric Hospital Adolescent Unit twelve years earlier. I wondered about their children.

Blodwen Morgan

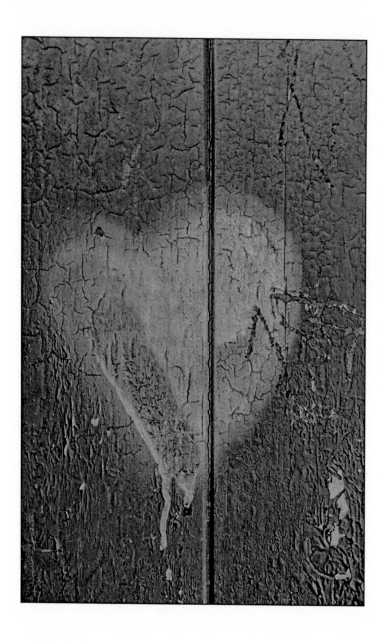

207

Visiting: Five By Five

On the far side of the field, at the edge
of the path, a man in shirt and tie, sleeves
rolled up, paces back and forth, back and forth,
one hand held to his head, the other gesturing
into the air, a claw gripping the emptiness

until it clicks – he's on his mobile, trying
to make sense, to get his message across:
his eyes turned inward to the business
of the phone, to the ears and voice on the other
end of the line, and his head nodding.

*

On the vinyl tiles, the tyre-marks squiggle
and veer towards the bolted doors.
Imagine the midnight wheelchair races
or the trundle of trolleys along the corridor
and the yells and screeches of laughing ghosts.

*

Through the window into West 5, flaking
walls, no bulbs in the fittings, loose wires
like question-marks. Empty beer bottles
from the final night. Who pressed the shackle
into the padlock? Who was last out?

*

His photograph shows him smiling up
at the camera from an archaeological trench
he'd dug. When they brought him here,
he never again recognised the gaze of other
eyes and never climbed out of the pit.

Robert Walton

I Sit Alone

I sit alone. My mint choc chip green and vanilla cream half
honeycomb shaped corridors empty; my dark wood
panelled heart heavy with the ambience of those who
stayed, wept, prayed, slept, and walked within.

I sit here alone. I wait for the builders, carpenters,
plumbers, and bulldozers to turn me and my grounds into
luxury flats, to open my strong walls and let out the scents
of Vaseline, wood polish, saddle soap, detergent, forgotten
foods – soaked into the walls, ceilings, floors.

I sit alone. I listen for the loud vibrating echoes and
muffled thumps of doors closing, keys turning, feet falling.
The quieter, secret sounds my inmates used to make.

I sit alone. I watch as vibrant green plants push against my
red-brick walls. Cobalt blue paint peels on wooden tables
and benches. Lichen consumes the once shiny black plastic
guttering while small, triangular voids fill up with bright
red hollyhocks, red carnations, green weeds, trapped,
desperate to get out.

I sit alone. Under the rain-grey sky, remembering the
sunny blues and cotton wool clouds of days gone by, the
laughter of children and staff alike; even the patients
joined in for a while.

I sit alone. I look out through the batwing leaded glass of
my fanlight. Now, all is quiet but for the chattering

magpies fending for themselves, alone amidst the soft sounds of paint peeling, plants creeping, moisture seeping beneath my eaves. And do I hear wheels, finally, coming up my cracked and scarred drive?

Midnight DeMaurisha

To an Edwardian Lady

You are surrounded by lawns that lie like Oxbridge playing fields. Sash windows, still stately, never really reflecting home. On your special birthday they dressed you in fresh paint, prepared you so your visitors would not be confronted with the indignity of your neglect. Like lipstick and rouge on an atrophied old lady, your resplendent red-brick walls attempt to conceal the decay of your inner sanctum. Your corridors display the passage of time as the trunk of a tree reveals its age; their nursery-coloured facade has become chipped, exposing old darker colours beneath. Plaques to honour ancient benevolence cling to your walls like sticking plasters. Age and neglect have made you sick to your heart, sustaining the obsolescence that will lead to your demise. Left to die in the detritus of those who have used or abused you, you have been denied the dignity of care in the community.

Jan Huyton

Four Weeks in Whitchurch

Emerging damaged from the car crash of my marriage, I moved from west Wales to Cardiff in 2001 for a new job; a new life.

Bipolar, lonely, and drinking heavily, it was only a matter of time before I ended up in Whitchurch Hospital, via a 999 call, a chat with a GP on night duty, and an ambulance ride.

My memory of my stay there is fragmentary. It must have been summer since I remember watching village cricket within the grounds. The place was geared up for sport; a bowling green, an old gymnasium, and a football pitch, where I would hide in the manager's dugouts, drinking illicit Czech lager bought from the corner shop across the road. My drinking didn't last long though. I'd been put on a detox programme (regular doses of valium to help with withdrawal) and I was told to stop, in no uncertain terms, by an aggressive nursing assistant as he pinned me to the wall. If my breath hinted alcohol I would be summarily discharged.

I had had spells in other Victorian asylums before, all of them, as they were planned, on the edges of towns, out of the sights and minds of the ordinary people. But Whitchurch was different in that it had been consumed by the city and dominated the area known as Whitchurch Village.

The building seemed deliberately labyrinthine, as if designed to disorientate the confused patient even further. I was frequently lost and had to ask for directions back to the acute ward, down one corridor and up a level.

I slept in a six – or eight – bedded dormitory, the beds separated only by curtains. This arrangement didn't lend itself to privacy or trust. There was a large lounge area, typical of other hospitals I'd stayed in, with a television, a pool table, a bookshelf, jigsaw puzzles, board games, and probably an aquarium. Fish are *so* calming!

I was very depressed and craved isolation and had little contact with my fellow patients but there were times when I would chain smoke with the rest of them in the brown, badly lit smoking room. If you smoke when admitted to a mental hospital, you'll smoke more because there is so much time to fill. If you don't smoke, you may well start.

There was a bright young student, affluent and outgoing. He would disappear all day to return at dinner time which was ridiculously early at six o'clock. He confided in me that he had a car parked in the grounds and he would drive around all day. The staff knew nothing of this. There were two prisoners from HMP Cardiff who had feigned illness in order to get a cushy change of routine from prison. Consequently the ward remained locked for the time they were there. They would get other patients to smuggle in vodka and get quietly drunk most nights.

There are two people I do remember. In places like this, by definition really, people behave outside the norm and you have to accept this and forgive bad behaviour. But there was one guy who I would have avoided altogether from the outset, were he not permanently encamped in the smoking room. He was vicious, rude, and menacing. A bully. I was actually afraid of him and it wouldn't surprise me if his diagnosis was 'advanced nastiness'.

On the other hand I did make friends with one of the guys. About my age, he was a lovely man who was a victim of the dance culture drugs scene. He always wore dungarees and had had been there for six months. Amusingly he was given to breaking out into dance moves, often when there was no music to be heard. From the very start he had stated that he was a vegetarian, yet more often than not his 'special diet' meal was not to be found on the food trolley and he was offered meat. I admired how he accepted this stoically and would take himself off to the kitchens to fetch his own meal. After I'd been discharged I invited him down to my local pub for Sunday blues music. It was a hollow experience. Outside the context of the hospital we had nothing in common.

I look back at my Whitchurch experience as a time of fear, desperation, and disorientation but when all things are considered it was simply a punctuation mark in the narrative of my life.

Anthony Jones

Sunday Best

Sunday afternoons in the 1950s were long and boring, especially during the winter. Sunday School over, one was usually taken to visit relatives and expected to behave quietly.

This mould was broken for me one January Sunday, 1958, when our family visited my grandfather, a patient at Whitchurch Hospital. This event was both exciting and scary. Having grown up with the looming landmark of the hospital water tower, we were familiar with local stories of locked doors and 'straight-jacketed' inmates. Now we would see for ourselves.

Anticipation mounted as we clacked along the endless corridor, up the stairs to the ward 'M1A.' My dad explained that 'M' stood for 'male.' All the wards on this side were 'men only.'

The ward door locked, we rang the bell which was soon answered by a welcoming nurse. I tiptoed along the gallery as we were ushered towards a homely lounge. There sat my granddad, asleep in an armchair next to a roaring coal fire. We were offered tea and biscuits, squash, and even ice cream 'for the children'! The atmosphere was warm and inviting, not even very quiet.

Over the several weeks we visited we learned a lot. My grandfather explained to us the nature of his treatment (ECT.). He spared no details as to the procedure. We took it in our stride.

We played cards and learned new card games from other patients and their families. It was fun. We were sad when our Sunday 'treat' came to an end, as all good things do. Glad, however, that Granddad came home and felt better.

I still use the tea tray he made in 'Occupational Therapy'.

Through the 1970s, when I worked at Whitchurch, staff not wearing a prescribed uniform donned white coats, usually pristine and freshly laundered. Doctors, pharmacists, charge-nurses, lab technicians, teaching staff were easily recognisable to each other, to patients, and to visitors.

How times have changed, along with attitudes regarding dress and staff/patient relationships. The white coat has all but disappeared from mental-health institutions. 'Men in white coats' became a negative cliché. 'Patients' are now more often referred to as 'clients'. Christian-name terms have become the norm.

My recollection is of a time when a sense of 'who's who' mattered. A boundary was drawn clearly between staff and patients who were, according to the Latin derivation, allowed to 'suffer' and, hopefully, to heal.

Anonymous

Serendipity

This piece was written after a recent visit to the hospital after an absence of about ten years.

This is a love story; one that was, for the most part, played out within the surrounds of Whitchurch Hospital. It is not the sort of love story that is the popular subject of romantic paperbacks – doctors and nurses, nurses and patients, patients and patients. No, this love story is about a quite different relationship; one built on serendipity.

He placed the palm of his hand flat against the window pane; believing for a moment that he could physically engage with the foliage on the other side. He had stood in this place many times before but now, as he gazed through the window, he could not remember the buddleia being as tall, or the brambles as thick and aggressive as now. He recalled that when he last looked through this window he could see across the triangular courtyard outside to the lawns beyond. Now the wild shrubs that before had been meticulously cultivated to confine their passage were forcing their way into the building, pressing against the glass of the windows and sending an occasional tendril through the gap beneath the door.

He should be sad, he thought. He should feel pain, or remorse, or longing, but he felt none of these. He knew that he would never get back what was. He just wanted to remember it.

The last time he was in this corridor, it was much busier. Staff hurried, some in uniforms, colour and style to denote their position in this place, some not. They would weave a carefully choreographed ballet around and between patients who had no reason to hurry. The place was like a village. People stood in groups, chatting or just waiting. Others peered through the shop window. Some laughed and others shouted.

Yes, he knew every inch of these corridors. He was not part of the medical staff; nor was he a patient, nor family. He wore a suit but he was not an accountant. They had met far from the hospital. They had talked and she asked, 'Do you know Whitchurch Hospital? I have just started there as an Occupational Therapist.' When the incredulity of the coincidence struck her, she said, 'a chance meeting of two perfect strangers and we find out we are working in the same place. What are the odds of that happening?'

'Serendipity,' he replied, 'the making of a pleasant discovery by accident.'

So he came to know the corridor in which he now stood. It was here that he would wait for her at the close of day. They would enjoy their precious time together; perhaps comparing their respective days, but more frequently not.

The door from the corridor to the OT department is locked now; as are most of the doors throughout the hospital – doors to offices, doors to cupboards, doors to wards, doors to minds. The sound of his footsteps bounced off the walls and preceded him down the corridor.

Nature has taken her now. She was the victim of nature's relentless invasion; the same nature that was now invading the fabric of the building. Soon the hospital would be gone. Then the names, and then the memories. Then, he thought, when all is forgotten, there will be a chance meeting with someone who *will* remember.

Serendipity.

James Wilson

Undergrowth

The edges of this sash window are freshly painted; a gloss of fireman red to frame my view. There is a garden of green outside. It is summer and the purple blossoms are fat, dangling; dried out by the heat. Their growth has continued unimpeded. The plants push up against the windows. There are brambles, competing with the flowers; pressing and pushing against the glass. The outside world has the illusion of being held back – but I close my eyes, and I am inside the tangle of weeds. The brambles catch at my T-shirt and pull at my hair. Something uncomfortable tickles my neck and elsewhere I feel a crawling up my leg. There is a musty, discomforting taste in my mouth. I hold my breath and begin to release it with short panting sounds. Opening my eyes brings some relief; but the undergrowth still presses. It feels claustrophobic against the glass; and yet contained. I breathe again. I begin to feel safer. I notice the thick solid walls of the hospital; the layers of brick which order the next layer. They are firm, upright, intact. The plants are held back.

Dr Sara MacBride-Stewart

Conkers

I must have been about eight or nine because I was at the age when conkers were like treasure. Spotting that chestnut shine in the grass was a thrill and I hoarded them in plastic bags under my bed until they became musty and covered in furry fungus.

My dad took me to Whitchurch Hospital one Saturday morning in October. He was a GP but must have had some work connection with the hospital or known someone who did. I felt like I had some special pass, putting me ahead of other conker-hunting boys in Cardiff, while at the same time feeling a bit like I was trespassing, aware that this wasn't a usual place for conker hunting. I was a conker poacher. I knew it was the 'mental' hospital and had been told that the patients who might be wandering in the grounds of the hospital might be chatty or funny. I don't think we saw anyone. I don't think I would have noticed because my attention was captured by the hundreds, thousands, it seemed millions, of brown diamonds littering the lawns beneath the horse chestnut trees. I filled my bags to the brim with conkers. They were good ones too. My favourites were those with one flat side and a sharp, clean edge. Was the fun taken out of conker hunting because of the amount available? Did I feel robbed of the excitement of the hunt or is that the sensible dad I am now talking? I think I was just delighted to have exclusive access to such rich pickings. We didn't go back another autumn but I remember the conker pick at Whitchurch Hospital as the most fruitful ever.

Gethin Wallace

Thirteen Missing

Beyond the gothic glass and tarnished brass of reception
remains the imprint of thirteen missing coat hooks, thirteen
missing coats, thirteen missing names, missing people.

Where the neon buzzes on peeling paintwork,

And battered walls sprout wires,

Like the tendrils of ivy that entwine the abandoned office
table in the courtyard,

Where yellowing Sellotape holds out-of-date notices,

And cigarette butts gather in the corners of unswept
walkways,

On a lino floor scarred by the wheels of once busy hospital
trolleys,

Doors stand fast under an array of locks. New locks, old
locks. Bolts of shining steel. Keyholes of tarnished brass.

Spied through a screen of wire-netted glass - a door hangs
limply on tired hinges. The crumbling ceiling weeps its
long, lifeless light cord down past the dirty pink walls to
the bare floorboards. Amongst the paint flakes, an empty
beer bottle. An iron bar.

Sighing with their stillness, amongst the silence of the rising damp, runs a quadrant of corridors.

But listen and you can still hear the beep of the lunch trolley, the jostle of keys and the slam of doors. Where tall linen trolleys shift, and swirl, and the artwork on the walls show recent dates. Somewhere, in that place, there is still a laugh. A voice. A long echo of footsteps.

Footsteps that lead to thirteen missing coat hooks, thirteen missing coats, thirteen missing names.
Missing people.

Jenny Ayres

Whitchurch Hospital

I still dream about Whitchurch Hospital forty-four years after working there. I began my nurse training in Whitchurch Hospital in January 1968 when I was twenty-one years of age. I qualified as a registered mental nurse three years later. I left Whitchurch Hospital in 1971 and I never returned.

In my dreams I walk the corridors, long and dark with wards leading off. Some of those wards were locked, keeping the world out and the patients in. I began my nurse training with no real idea about the work I would be required to do, no idea about the responsibilities I would have, and certainly no idea about the people that I would be expected to care for. Those people, mostly the elderly ladies on what was then called the pycho-gereatric wards, would shape the rest of my life and I know I will remember them always.

I'm not sure why I made the decision to train as a psychiatric nurse. I never planned on being a nurse, I never really planned on being anything. I read poetry, philosophy, and the works of Sigmund Freud. I naively imagined that a psychiatric hospital was in some way like the books I had read, a place of ideals where people understood one another and where people cared about one another and a place where everyone was accepted for who they were. How wrong could I be? Everyone had said I wasn't the type to be a nurse, I disagreed, so, there I was, with too much pride to go home and admit I had made a mistake. I was frightened, but I stayed.

My parents drove me to the hospital on December 31st

1967, New Year's Eve. I was to start my training on Jan 1st

My father was unhappy; he never wanted me to do this, I would be better off in all ways, working in the GPO factory, he said. My mother said that I should do what I wanted, and I wanted to do this. God knows why!

Whitchurch Hospital, a sprawling building on the outskirts of Whitchurch Village, an institution which in the 1960s still retained some remnants of the way it had been years earlier. In the 1960s there were some bits of the farm buildings left where patients had grown vegetables and kept chickens. There was a chapel in the grounds and we escorted the patients there on a Sunday.

The lecturers in Whitchurch were nurses, psychiatrists, and psychologists, all of them trying to prepare us for the reality of caring for mentally ill people. It was nothing like I expected. Where were the couches and the talking therapies, where were the psychoanalysts? Certainly not in Whitchurch, and that was a fact. Freud and his theories were not a part of Whitchurch Hospital, the name of the game was drug therapy, chemical straightjackets in the form of Stelazine and Largactil, major tranquilisers, whose side effects were as bad if not worse than the original illness, along with electroconvulsive therapy, and for good measure a dose or two of insulin therapy.

I remember nameless and faceless patients. Some had been there for ever, shuffling along the corridors, smoking their cigarettes, some with a limp, caused, I was told, by ECT treatments, which years before had been so invasive as to break bones. These patients were chronic schizophrenics (burnt out) was the term used. Others had apparently undergone lobotomies. Hundreds of patients lobotomized for who knows what. That had stopped by 1968.

One ward which had a lasting impression upon me remains clear in my mind: the female disturbed ward. It was always locked. Students had to do placement there.

Each morning during that placement when we entered the ward, the ward sister would say 'dayroom'. That meant you went to the dayroom and you stayed there with the patients. I can never remember the ward sister leaving her office. The psychiatrist, I remember, was female, and she would enter the ward by a side door and go straight to sister's office, where they would sit together. I never remember her coming to the dayroom either, but perhaps my memory fails me.

I remember one patient vividly, she was about sixty-five years of age when I made her acquaintance, and she had been in Whitchurch since the age of nineteen. For most of those years she had been violent and locked in her room, only coming out under escort. Every morning we would take her breakfast, unlock her door, and call her name. Either a glare or a leap out of the bed would determine what happened to her breakfast. The quicker you left her room the better.

Rows upon rows of beds, beds low to the ground, no more than mattresses really, housing nameless elderly ladies suffering with dementia. Beds to be made, patients (not people) to be toileted, washed, and put in chairs. Fed and watered, no more; I can't remember a single conversation with one of them, or a name or a face. I remember the ward sister, not her name, just her uniform: dark blue with stiff white collar and cuffs. I remember damp dusting the lockers and polishing the floors. I remember standing to say prayers every morning. We should have prayed for the souls we cared for but I don't think we did. I do that now.

ECT was every week, patients would be strapped to the trolley and the student nurses would lie across their bodies and hold them down while an electric shock was delivered to their brain. Their bodies would rise up as if in protest, and we would press down even harder to hold them. When it was over we would take them back to the wards and sit with them until they regained consciousness.

I was a second year student nurse. I had to work nights. My first experience was to be in charge of an acute admission ward. Nights will never be as long as they were then: twelve-hour shifts, alone, frightened. I found this very difficult to cope with and admitted my fears to my parents and my GP. My parents begged me to leave, but I wouldn't and so a letter was written to the hospital and I was then moved to complete my stint of night duty on the psycho-geriatric ward.

My memories are vivid and still remain with me over forty years on. There was a fireplace and by the time the dawn broke there would be several elderly ladies sitting around the fireplace alongside me. The night was a constant round of what was so eloquently called 'wet rounds': this entailed changing soiled sheets, whilst at the same time trying to keep the patients in their beds until the morning came.

I had a nursing auxiliary to help me, but reality was, she disappeared as soon as she came on duty and I never saw her until the next morning. There were many stories about her exploits. All I knew, she was never there to help me. I would start the 'wet round' at 5 a.m.. This meant getting these elderly ladies out of bed, washed, and dressed by the time the day staff came on duty. I still think about them, and know that I failed them through ignorance and lack of support. I complained to my managers and got nowhere.

Another ward which stays with me was a female psycho-geriatric ward. A new ward sister was employed; I was a student nurse at the time. It was the routine that at breakfast time the patients would sit at tables and their tea would be poured out of big teapots into their cups. The new ward sister made changes. We were told to put hot tea into teapots onto the tables with milk and sugar in respective containers. Sadly a bridge too far; it didn't work. Ladies drank from the teapots. She was redeployed and we went back to the way it was before.

Three years after beginning my training I qualified as a registered mental nurse. I had a choice of wards. I was asked would I like to work on the professorial unit; this was a bit of an elite. I said no thanks. I wanted to work on the pycho-gereatric ward. My managers thought I was mad. 'Why would you want to do that?' they asked. I knew why, and I am glad to this day that I did. As a staff nurse I was able to make changes and I took pride in being able to help these ladies have a better quality of life for the time they had left.

There were many challenges on this ward, but there were many good times, sitting with the ladies at tea-time, tucking them into bed at night, helping them to remember what they couldn't remember, reassuring them when they cried for their mothers or their husbands who were long gone.

In the early 1970s the University Hospital of Wales opened with a psychiatric unit. I was asked would I like to go to work on the professorial unit at the new hospital and I accepted. From there I went into general nursing. I never returned to Whitchurch, only in my dreams.

Judith Allen

Strange Experiences

A considerable number of people seem to have had strange experiences at the hospital, which are difficult to explain.

One dark evening a colleague asked me if I had 'felt anything strange' near the entry to the west corridor. He certainly had. Only ten minutes before he spoke to me. He had also experienced it many times before. I realised that I had often felt uncomfortable when I was in this section of the hospital: a feeling that something wasn't quite right, plus a desire to quicken my pace and glance over my shoulder. I then discovered that many people had had this experience and that it was associated with an old story (which I had been told many years before but had forgotten).

It appears that for decades, staff working at night, and passing through that area had sometimes seen a grey mistiness which occasionally resolved into shape resembling an Edwardian lady wearing a long grey dress plus sort of headgear. The old matrons' office was adjacent. I never experienced it myself, but over the last century several hundred people have claimed to.

There is a back area between two wards which is avoided as much as possible by staff, especially at night, but also during day time. The area simply contains a stairway to the first floor, various cupboards, and an emergency exit. Many staff have complained of panic and terror in this place when they have experienced a non-existing person tapping them on the shoulder.

I have had many minor experiences of this sort whilst on night duty but always dismissed them as being due to tiredness and momentary hallucinations. However, two incidents defy explanation.

One night in 1990 I was sitting at a desk in a ward office concentrating on completing a document. I heard an elderly male patient who was known to me, making his way from his bed in the male dormitory towards the toilet area. The noises accompanying his journey were always the same: the dormitory door would make its distinctive opening sound, he would clump his way toward the other door, which also had its familiar cracking noise, and would close it behind him with an annoying bang. I remember thinking, 'gosh, he's early tonight' and then 'freezing' as I realised that there were no male patients on the ward – they had all been sent home for the weekend.

I stepped out of the office to find the two (female) ward nurses nearby both looking 'shaken'. I asked them if they had heard what I had and they both nodded yes. Together we scoured the ward but found no male patient. The male dormitory was empty and all the beds unslept in. The male toilet area was mostly locked, but I unlocked and checked everywhere. This man's 'clunky' sounding walk was very distinctive and was due to his refusal to use slippers. He went back and forth in unlaced shoes.

On another occasion, in the mid 1980s, I was standing at the junction of two corridors discussing something with a doctor. As we talked I noticed a movement at the entrance to the hospital main kitchens halfway down one of the corridors – a considerable distance from me. A man dressed in what looked like white overalls (kitchen staff clothing) seemed to be wandering back and forth. It was 3.15 a.m and no kitchen staff were on duty. The doctor went on her way and I started to walk towards the person in white. I came to a halt when he walked towards the opposite wall and simply walked *into* it. I carried on walking towards him with my eyes trained on the spot where he had vanished. When I got there, no man, of course, existed. Just a blank wall. No doorway or window. I checked the kitchen doors – all were secure. The doctor later launched into a long discussion about hallucinations, suggestibility, and tiredness.

Keith Sullivan

Cold Walls

Cold building.
Cold walls.
Traumatic soldiers in the Second World War.
Whispering of wandering ghosts.
Artificial plants on the dirty walls.
Closed doors in the horrific corridors.
Notes of longing on the walls;

'I WANT J'

J's who have been forgotten 'here' are people who think
about them!

One corridor to another.

Corridors of loneliness,
Corridors of tears,
Corridors of shrieks,
Corridors of fear.

Suddenly;

      A curving corridor.
                A corridor like the arcade!

Arcade of
      Yellow,
         Sweet,
            Big,
              Juicy pears

in a crowded Bazaar of Shahpour,
in Tehran,
in a hot midday of summer.

Feeling good!

Let these cold walls turn into the luxury flats.

Then,

happiness replaces
all the history of sadness and darkness.

Mitra Sanei Moghaddam

Night Duty

Alone again. Quietness, just muffled sounds as I walk the long corridors.

Not really alone, of course, just appears to be so after the coming and going of a busy day. The wards are mostly full, and there are two allotted staff each. Then there is the night porter, seeming to me to be keeping watch over the main front doors of the hospital in his small office, as well as manning the switchboard which connects the outside world, and the wards, to my bleep.

I look down at the red display in my pocket and ring the ward. I am needed to access some medicine from the pharmacy.

There are no staff in the hospital pharmacy at night. I remember advice given to me by my medical predecessor and realise that this is the time to put his words into practice. I unlock the door carefully and open the door just sufficiently to slip my arm through to find the light switch. Suddenly there is an amazingly loud scuttling noise as cockroaches run to find a place of darkness.

When all is quiet, I open the door fully and, by trial and error, with various keys, obtain what is needed without having to crunch on any of those pests. I notice one, before I leave, with his long antennae waving and I imagine his biting mouthparts and shudder.

Eventually I decide that I might try and get some sleep and head for the on call room upstairs. Heavily pregnant it is a joy to put my feet up at last.

I am not sure how long I was asleep but am woken by the sound of breaking glass. The porter must have heard this too, as he rings me having gone to investigate. He advises I lock the room and stay put for the present as someone has broken into the pharmacy.

There are no further calls in the early hours and finally the dawn rises for another new day over the grounds of Whitchurch Hospital.

Dr Elizabeth Thomas

The Hat

Jim, my father, had a favourite hat. It was Bavarian green. He always seemed happy to put it on his head. It echoed the green of his eyes, and his big personality.

At the funeral, held during the austere, Anglican time of Lent, my greatest wish was for the hat to sit on his coffin during his funeral and the Requiem Mass. It did.

Now, it resides on my mother's coffee table.

Something is taking me away
Far beyond the places I have always known
Somebody has taken all my clothes
Replacing them with those I do not own

My hat is mine
It sits upon my head
A crown of continuity

Thoughts are very hard to order now
Understanding the present is thankless role
History is easier to wear
Such comfort from my youthful, healthy soul

My hat is mine
It fits my head just so
A symbol of our unity

Peggy bought a Valentine to sign with my love
Three little kisses and my name she asked of me
I signed my name three times with one small kiss
A little private joke, Peg, for you to see

My hat was mine
It fit me properly
Before I found eternity

Jane King

The Postgraduate Medical Education Centre

I was told about Whitchurch Postgraduate Medical Centre soon after I came to work in Cardiff in the spring of 1969. It had been built behind the main hospital buildings offering good facilities and, perhaps most importantly, a large car park with fairly easy access to the road network of South Wales.

Doctors came to Whitchurch from Gwent, South Glamorgan, and Mid and West Glamorgan to listen to visiting experts and to discuss their own ways of working. It was where we went regularly to meet colleagues and to keep in touch with developments in medical care.

In 1990 the centre was extended. Several Portakabins were added to provide an office base for 'Teamcare Valleys'. This was a project led by the College of Medicine in Cardiff, supported by the Welsh Office, with the aim of developing teamwork in the general practices based in the South Wales valleys. Doctors, nurses, health visitors, and practice managers went out to visit all health centres and clinics in the area which stretched from Pontypool in the east to Ammanford in the west. They returned to Whitchurch to share their experiences, to seek expert advice, and to develop plans for a range of projects before returning to work with their colleagues in primary care throughout the former South Wales coalfield.

The centre was a hive of activity for three years, and then the funds ran out. Reports were written and people moved on but memories and contacts have been maintained.

Dr Brian Wallace

Tŷ Canol

Tŷ Canol was the café at the centre of Whitchurch Hospital. It would open around 1 p.m. in the afternoons, just after lunch, and some evenings. Such was its popularity that often, in the afternoons, there would be a queue of people waiting to get in before it opened.

Although quite small, it was a friendly, warm, inviting place – there was usually music playing and the staff – both paid and voluntary – would always have time to talk to you.

Tea or coffee was exceptionally cheap – perhaps 30-40p – and there was even the slightly quaint offer of 5 or 10p back for returning cups or mugs.

There was a mini pool table – probably four foot – which was very popular. Sometimes a tournament would be held in the evenings, and these were hotly contested. If you spent a lot of time in the hospital, you really could become pretty good at the game – a lot of the wards also had pool tables on them. The nurses, some of whom must have got even more practice, were often almost impossible to beat.

There were a couple of computers which patients were allowed to use, but actually, patients did not use these all that much. Not when I was there last anyway, which was about eight years ago (around 2006). It may be different now, but quite possibly not, as I think a lot of people who went to Whitchurch would not necessarily be the sort of people who would use computers all that much. There was internet access, but there were not many people using the internet, although this was before Facebook became popular.

Personally, I mostly used the computers to type up poetry. Whenever I have been unwell, and especially when in hospital, I have been incredibly prolific when it comes to poetry. A lot of it might not make all that much sense, but I would find myself writing poem after poem. I think when I had my last admission, I had written perhaps fifty poems in the lead up to being admitted, and then continued to write several more once I was sectioned. So I had reams and reams of the stuff, and I used the computers at Tŷ Canol to type it up and store it.

Bear in mind that doing anything like this while in hospital was not easy though. Most people, including myself, would be quite heavily medicated. Simply typing up a poem would require quite a lot of effort, so managing to type up enough to make a small book of poems was quite an achievement for me. As I say, a lot of the poems written at that time may not make that much sense now, but had quite a bit of significance at the time!

Nick Fisk

Day after Day

An escort wherever I go,
like guards escorting prisoners about the place.
Medication they give you
with regular ease
take one take two or maybe more.
They make you feel better.
Coming and going the hospital goes on
while you sit on a chair and stare.
You see no hope, no dreams, no future you see.
Whiling away the time,
day after day
but slowly the words seem to make sense
and gradually you move
from the chair to the gym.
You ask to go – and you are not forced.
Some small pleasures begin and grow.
Now you speak to the nurses and doctors
You seek their help.
As time goes past – you see a future.
The workings of the hospital
now make sense.
You ask for the help
and day by day you go further,
they let you out by yourself.
Freedom at last, home is near.
You leave the hospital, cured?
Or not.

Tracy Hartwell

One Day in the Madhouse

I am sitting at a table laid with knives and forks
And stare out of smoky windowpanes where
One can see the patients going for walks.
I feel depressed as the nurses call for us to get medication
When I take them I notice how my face shone,
Restless patients, asking questions, staring at me with
worried looks
As I stroll over to a corner looking at books.
What has happened to my concentration?
That is what I think as I pull out my ration
Of cigarettes which I smoke by the dozen
No one comes to see me, not even a cousin.
Beds in a row, lonely, waiting for their occupants
It's 'Hell on Earth' one patient rants.
Locked doors depicting the hopelessness of the place
I want to hide as I see another staring face.
The gardens below are neatly mowed
The high fence separates the insane from the sane in the
road.
Birds fly outside singing as if nothing is wrong
While thoughts beat in my head, it's to be as free as a bird
I do long.
As I try and keep still I hope they will go away
And never come back not even on a rainy day!
I long to go home and see my family
I want to be back with them, quite naturally
Perhaps one day they will let me go
Alas – when, I do not know.

Shane V Simons

Poem previously published in This Sacred World anthology edited by Joanne Baxton (Poetry Now, Peterborough)

A Place of Contradiction

As an SRN student in the late 1970s, Whitchurch Hospital was not a place to which I wanted to go. I was apprehensive because it represented a particular form of the unknown. To go there meant encountering unfamiliar expressions of ill health and having to deliver equally unfamiliar care, while the place also carried an undeniable stigma associated with its purpose. A few patients for whom I'd cared in general hospitals had needed to be 'sent' there once their physical health improved; some had gone gratefully and others with fearful reluctance. It didn't help that my only prior sightings had been of old photographs. Dominated by a looming tower, the stark images reinforced an impression of Whitchurch as foreboding and as an asylum in the negative sense. The site was shown bounded by fences and its buildings huddled away from the road, together marking out an institutional detachment from the world around it.

'General nurses' weren't required to gain experience in mental health but I chose the option offered, conscious that I would meet people with related problems wherever I worked. Pre-placement classes were held in the hospital's nondescript modern school block, the leader in a casual jacket instead of our usual male tutors' suited style. Session presentation mirrored this refreshing informality but content was still ordered; we studied named conditions and their itemised clinical features. There seemed a drive to categorise; to define patients by diagnostic labels, so that treatment could be determined and its side effects treated in turn. Talk then was of psychiatry, not mental

246

health; patients, not service users; behavioural disturbance, not emotional distress; treatment, not recovery; and disorders, not the lived experiences of people who had them. Patients were seen compassionately but through the lens of their illness; talk was of 'them' as if separate from 'us'.

The hospital complex stood for me as a place of contradiction. The gatehouse and chapel gave the appearance of an Edwardian estate, though the health authority's branded sign signified public ownership. The main building's red and cream banded brick was both hard and easy on the eye: its solidity suggesting custodial threat and sanctuary simultaneously. The wide arch of its elegant pillared entrance and expansive cultivated green spaces surrounding it evoked a sense of freedom, the tightly paned windows and closed doors the opposite.

The hospital's definitive feature was its disorienting warren of corridors, brick inside as well as out; painted here, yet gloomy and oppressive on a typically dull Cardiff day; their angled ceilings bearing down and unending walls interrupted by sash windows which I suspected could not be opened and would be deemed inappropriate if tried. Staff in street clothes moved along the corridors purposefully. Less attentively dressed patients wandered, aimless, and as if filling in time. Some raised weary eyes to ask for cigarettes, not really hearing my mumbled apology that I didn't smoke.

In that pre-placement period, sanity and madness seemed distinct. I hadn't yet learned of the spectrum of mental health, or that our shared humanity and the labours of caring for lost minds meant that 'them' and 'us' were actually 'we', but I was learning other things. I learned that, although nurses didn't wear uniform to avoid it acting as a barrier between staff and patients, there were other, less obvious, barriers present in this new world. I learned that the simple act of acknowledging a patient in the corridor could be meaningful; an undemanding link to 'normal' when illness otherwise distanced them from life's interactions or made these effortful. I learned that, despite the hospital now feeling less strange, its corridors left me uneasy. My fingers remained crossed that my placement would be elsewhere. I was relieved to find that it was. Whitchurch was still not a place to which I wanted to go.

Erica Alabaster

Going Back

When I was freed from my section – the day before it was due to end – I felt a bit lost in the outside world. I popped back occasionally, to visit patients who had become friends and to buy the home-made cakes. I even went back for shoes – cheaper and more practical than the commercial rates.

But when I was readmitted it was awful – I felt I'd let the other patients down. My section was six months – I could be forced to take drugs. And I was.

I was released after three months.

When I got out that time, I didn't go back.

Marilyn Kemeny

Needs

I a̶ ̶shelter but in order to protect those I shelter, I must be ̶ ̶too.
I am a nu̶r̶ ̶ but in order to nurture others, I must be nurtured.
I am a healer, but in orde̶r̶ ̶to heal, I must be healed myself.

I have relied on my faith in others to protect me, nurture me and heal me.
Sometimes I have been cared for but I have also been neglected and abused.
I stood face to face with the church and it was my witness.
It has now been deconsecrated.

There are stains on my floors, wildlife beating at my doors,
paint peeling, blistered walls and ceilings,
overflowing rubbish bins, discarded beer cans.

I was built as an asylum.
I have grown into a shelter, a nurturer, a healer.
I am 100 years old but I didn't receive a letter from the queen.
Now I am being retired.

Hollie Edwards-Davies

Departure

My first work experience of Whitchurch was during the day on the extreme east of the hospital. My last was at night on the extreme west. I had been preparing for this moment for some time: taking many photographs and venturing to the top of the water tower and down into the crypt that runs like a network under the hospital. Increasing amounts of time were being spent wandering around the old place, stopping for a few moments here and there to ponder on what it had all been about. Doors, gardens, grounds, wall recesses, corners, offices, discussion rooms: all had great meaning and all reminded me of past events.

I walked to the exit door at the western end and paused in the porch. Behind me, sounds drifted up the corridor: the rattle of someone's keys, a snatch of laughter, a door slamming somewhere and distant voices. And also footsteps. The corridors always seemed to echo with footsteps and as I stood there, I thought of the enormous distances I had covered tramping those corridors and of the large number of people who had accompanied me. Some had been called patients. Others had been called hospital staff. I had friends in both departments.

And then I found myself thinking of the thousands of people who had found shelter and comfort and succour in that strange building ever since it opened its door. I was, of course, one of those people. I never knew the vast majority of the others and never knew their stories and never would, but it was comforting to realise that I had played my part in helping them, or at least, a few of them.

251

I stepped out into the early morning sunshine. The gardens and grounds looked beautiful. It was late August. There were two woodpeckers in a nearby tree. I strolled through the grounds for the final time, taking it all in. Then I went home.

Keith Sullivan

The Editors

Phil Carradice has published over 50 books, including fiction, poetry, history (both local and national), travel, and biographies. He has edited several anthologies and is one of the editors of *Roundyhouse* poetry magazine. Phil also writes a weekly blog for BBC History and regularly leads creative writing sessions for children and adults. He has recently been commissioned to write twelve books on the Royal Navy in World Wars I and II. Phil is on the Literature Wales Board of Directors and is a Fellow of The Welsh Academy. A native of Pembroke Dock, he now lives with his wife Trudy in the Vale of Glamorgan.

Briony Goffin teaches creative writing at The Centre for Lifelong Learning at Cardiff University and is an experienced practitioner in facilitating creative writing experiences for adults and young people with mental health problems. She has run writing courses and one-off sessions for the NHS, Cardiff Council, Literature Wales, Age Cymru, HMP Parc, Cardiff People First, Sky Arts, and The Hay Festival. Briony has published and spoken widely on the art of teaching creative writing and supporting student writers to fulfil their creative potential. In 2012, she was named 'Inspirational Tutor of the Year' by NIACE Dysgu Cymru.

For more information about

Accent Press titles

please visit

www.accentpress.co.uk

For news on Accent Press authors and upcoming titles
please visit

http://accenthub.com/

Lightning Source UK Ltd.
Milton Keynes UK
UKOW02f2215081114

241321UK00002BA/20/P